OUTLAW

OUTLAW

How I Became Britain's Most Wanted Man

RAY BISHOP

Foreword by
Noel 'Razor' Smith

2 4 6 8 10 9 7 5 3 1

Published in 2014 by Virgin Books, an imprint of Ebury Publishing

A Random House Group Company

Copyright © Ray Bishop 2014

Ray Bishop has asserted his right under the Copyright, Designs and Patents Act 1988 to be identified as the author of this work

The Random House Group Limited Reg. No. 954009

Addresses for companies within the Random House Group can be found at www.randomhouse.co.uk

A CIP catalogue record for this book is available from the British Library

The Random House Group Limited supports the Forest Stewardship Council® (FSC®), the leading international forest-certification organisation. Our books carrying the FSC label are printed on FSC®-certified paper. FSC is the only forest-certification scheme supported by the leading environmental organisations, including Greenpeace. Our paper procurement policy can be found at www.randomhouse.co.uk/environment

Printed and bound in Great Britain by Clays Ltd, St Ives PLC

ISBN 9780753555668

To buy books by your favourite authors and register for offers visit www.randomhouse.co.uk

For Sammy and Poppy, for teaching me
the true meaning of love

'In my opinion, Mr Bishop is a young man desperately seeking avenues of communication'

DR R.M. BELL, HOME OFFICE
CONSULTANT PSYCHIATRIST

CONTENTS

FOREWORD

I first met Ray Bishop in HMP High Down back in the 1990s when he was deep into his world of violence and addiction. He was pointed out to me by another south London face, who informed me that Ray was up-and-coming in the criminal world and was 'as game as a bag of rabid pit bulls'. The only trouble was that he was also an addict. Never a good combination. At this time I was a confirmed career criminal serving a very long sentence and engaged in my own mad battle against the forces of law and order, so I viewed Ray as a fellow traveller on the same road.

The next time I met Ray was when I walked into HMP Grendon in the summer of 2003. I was serving a life sentence and Ray was looking at a decade behind bars. It seems we had separately reached much the same conclusion – that we had had enough of crime and punishment and wanted to try and change our lives.

Grendon was a hard journey but Ray took to the therapeutic regime and used it to stay clean of drugs and learn as much about the origins of his own destructive behaviour as he could. The theory is that once you have recognised where you have been going wrong then you can take steps to not repeat the same behaviour again. It works, but with those who have an addictive personality it becomes a full-time job.

Our time at HMP Grendon allowed me to see another side of Ray. I found out he wasn't just another addicted criminal wannabe but a bright, articulate and funny man who, whilst sober and clear of drugs, understood his addiction very well. The trouble for Ray was the times when his addiction took over. It was then that you would want to steer well clear of Ray Bishop.

I lost touch with Ray once he had left prison but was very much surprised and pleased to hear that he had written this book. I knew that Ray could speak well, but I know plenty of people who can speak well and that doesn't mean they are able to articulate their thoughts through the written word; putting a book together is a particular skill that requires concentration and dedication.

So I was pleasantly surprised that once I started reading I could not put the book down. Unlike the majority of criminal memoir writers, Ray does not give it the big 'I am', nor even the big 'I was'; instead, he documents the real fear, depression and paranoia that come when you dedicate your life to crime and imprisonment. He explains the reality of being so strung out on drugs that when you actually hit rock bottom you no longer care what happens to you; the desperation of having nothing but a drug habit to keep you getting up in the mornings.

The writing is so vivid that you feel as though you are living it with him – from the lows of being caught smuggling illegal immigrants into the country, to the highs of winning his super-middleweight British boxing title.

Let's be clear about this, Ray Bishop has a lot to say about addiction, mental health and the criminal justice system in this country and, as this is coming from someone with a vast experience of these subjects, the so-called experts should take note. This is a book that should be required reading for all those involved in these areas in Britain, because although Ray Bishop was strong enough and determined enough to beat his addictions and come out the other side a better man, many are not. This book might offer a clue on how to help them.

Ray Bishop is a true champ who refused to go down, no matter what life hit him with.

NOEL 'RAZOR' SMITH

PREFACE

The long dark night will eventually give birth to the brightness of dawn. Any once-troubled soul who has found redemption will understand this statement. The frailty of the human condition means that we all face our own Everest at some point in our lives. Reaching the summit and seeing above the clouds is our moment of triumph. In the end it was worth the steepest of climbs as we are reborn and taste a new freedom.

Please allow me to introduce myself. My name is Ray Bishop, and I am a reformed criminal and a recovering addict. My life before rehabilitation was one of immense destruction, to both myself and others. In the grip of addiction, I operated in a world of organised crime such as drug smuggling and people trafficking. Much to my regret at one point I was also one of a team of armed robbers who were described by the police – correctly – as extremely prolific.

I make no excuses for my selfish actions when I was criminally active. I am not proud of them and I have gone to great lengths to become the reformed person that I am today.

I pray that my redemption goes in some small way in recompense to those I have harmed.

I am in several books already for my various exploits but I have never told my own story. Razor Smith describes me in his book *A Rusty Gun* as being too crazy for my own good. I would describe myself as being too stupid at times to learn from my own mistakes.

I have been told that to not tell my story is a crime in itself, as it may be an inspiration to anyone who is struggling to turn their life around. This is a compliment that I am not sure that I deserve. So with some reservations I have decided to give it a go and tell my tale in my own words.

In changing my ways I have become an educated man and have been crime-free for quite some time. I also won a UK boxing title when not many gave me a chance. My greatest success is that I dedicate much of my time today to trying to help men like me reform. This is the main purpose of me writing this book. If I can change from being a hopeless criminal drug addict, then maybe this will inspire someone else. It has taken a long time but I openly admit today that there is no such thing as victimless crime.

While in prison I gained a degree in psychology and I also have a diploma in alcohol and drug counselling. My knowledge has enabled me to examine my own motives and in this book I share some of my own views and opinions in relation to my experiences. Feel free to agree or disagree, as I am by no means an expert on anything. I do not profess to have all the answers. I do, however, claim that I have found many of my own in the process of retracing my life.

My life experience is that I have spent many years behind bars and I have also taken part in many treatment programmes. I have completed rehabilitation courses and I once spent three years in a therapeutic community. This was as a result of my violence in prison where I came close to receiving a life sentence. My behaviour before my treatment can only be described as dangerous and insane.

The nature of my own untreated condition is that I once suffered a drug-induced psychosis. In this state I escaped from prison and became one of Britain's most wanted men. The public were warned not to approach me on several news channels. On my recapture I was kept in solitary confinement for almost a year in a high-security unit and not allowed any human contact.

In this story of my life I pull no punches and my accounts are both graphic and tragic. I have been fighting my whole life and I have described with honesty my own psychological battles. I have really tried to encapsulate the insanity of my own thinking in relation to my addiction and crimes. I have also tried my best to convey in detail what it felt like to be in prison for long periods of time. For me this became lonely and painful and propelled me to face up to the reality of life in a criminal wasteland.

Rehabilitation has not come easy for me. I have faced my own Waterloo many times along the way and have tried and failed on numerous occasions to change my ways. Each time

I have learned many valuable lessons and been able to draw on them to better my chances. As my condition progressed, I gradually became more and more encased in my own fractured mind. Paradoxically speaking, I have had to get worse to eventually get better.

Writing this book is not an attempt to gain sympathy or to glamorise crime in any way. For me, a dishonest lifestyle did not pay, and I have much cause for regret. I have damaged many people, and if I could undo this harm, I would. There have been times when I have bowed my head during the writing of this book. I too have paid a heavy price for my actions and I am not the man today that once I was.

This book is also not about trying to gain an image or a reputation. If I give this impression when describing some of my life events, it was never my intention. There is nothing clever about committing crime and creating victims. You will see why I feel like this as you read through my life. This is an honest book and I hope it encourages others to face their demons as I have.

It has been enormously emotional retracing the lonely roads that I once walked down. I have relived the insanity I once felt and gained a better degree of empathy with those I have hurt along the way. However painful it has been, writing my book has proved to be an incredibly rewarding experience. Now that it's done I pray that my sleep pattern can return to a semi-normal state. I have achieved what I have struggled with my whole life. I have become honest and stepped out from behind my addictions and the criminal masks that were destroying me.

Today I am a free man who has earned the right to look the world in the eye through my own continuous rehabilitation. I hope anyone who follows my journey throughout this book may come to understand people like me. I am by no means unique, as there are many more just like I once was.

I present to you the chaos that was my life. It is a graphic account of addiction and serious crime. I have created many victims and for that I am deeply ashamed. I am a guilty man who deserved all he got, whereas those affected by my madness did not. What a long and destructive journey it has been to date, and I would change many things if I could.

I certainly would change the harms I have caused my loved ones and society at large. I would change all the wasted years in prison and suffering in emotional silence. I would change the fact that I have committed many criminal acts in addiction and above all the fact that I have harmed people physically. The one thing I cannot change is my past, but what I do today will change my future.

Please allow me to take you on a journey into my former dark world. Together we will make it back to shore safely. I need to share a story with you, and that story is my own.

RAY BISHOP

'DO NOT APPROACH THIS MAN'

They say that everybody wants to be on television. Well, I don't think this was what they had in mind.

I was sitting in a dealer's house in Plumstead, south-east London, waiting to get my fix. And to be honest with you, I had a lot that I needed to escape from – not least the fact that I was a career criminal who was currently on the run from the law.

That very morning, 15 May 2000, I had been taken by prison wagon, or sweatbox as us regular inhabitants called them, to Folkestone Magistrates' Court. I was due to be committed to Maidstone Crown Court – and I knew that, after they had gone through the motions of a trial, I was facing a fucking horribly long jail sentence.

The charge I was facing was not a light one: being know-ingly concerned with the facilitation of thirty human beings into the United Kingdom. Or, to put it in layman's terms: people trafficking. A few days earlier I had got caught driv-ing a Volvo lorry with a hidden cargo of thirty East European would-be illegal immigrants into a small French town called Coquelles, just outside Calais, en route to Ashford in Kent.

I hadn't felt good about the job – it had seemed like a mistake from the start – and my misgivings had been justi-fied when I pulled up in the port to be greeted by a reception committee of French cops and customs officers. I never stood a chance.

The French cops had given me shit, both personally and because of my nationality, which I had not taken well as I am a patriotic man. Sitting in Canterbury Prison a few days later, in a single cell as always because of my violent prison history, I knew that I couldn't face a long stretch inside.

Feeling myself slipping back into the mental black hole that has so often consumed me, and sweating for the opiates that I needed but couldn't get behind bars, my mind had led me to a twisted conclusion.

I would have to escape.

Well, easier said than done … or was it?

The prison officer who searched me as I was shipped out of Canterbury Prison into the sweatbox to court had hardly noticed the paper clip holding my court papers together. Nor did he care about my plastic Bic biro, or the blackcurrant jam sandwich that I was casually eating as I was frisked.

They looked what they were, three innocuous items – but I knew that they were the keys to my cage.

At the magistrates' court, I had made it my business to be extra-nice to the court staff dealing with me. You know what they say in the Mafia: murderers come with smiles. Nothing induces terror so much as a warm, friendly face that hardens in a second into a vicious monster.

I had worked fast in the cell area, ripping the biro in half with my teeth and filling it with the blackcurrant jam. Once I had put the straightened-out paper clip in the top of the pen, it looked enough like a blood-filled syringe to terrify anyone whose quivering neck it was rammed against.

I stashed it in the waistband of my jeans, and waited.

When the two jailers had arrived to escort me to the hearing, I had joked with them all the way to the courtroom – right until we stepped into the dock with its glass casing. At which point I had grabbed one of them, slapped the syringe to his throat, and threatened to inject him if any-one moved.

His mate had tried to reason with me but one look into my eyes told him that I meant business. He opened the door to the dock and I fled from the courtroom – after first locking everybody in with the keys I had just nicked from the guards.

Now instinct and adrenaline took over as I jumped over a garden wall and stole a jumper off a washing line to wear as a disguise. I knew the police would be looking for anyone running away from the court building, so I doubled back and headed towards the beach.

As a police helicopter hovered overhead, I noticed a woman in her twenties, like me, sitting on a bench with a small child in a pram. I went over and introduced myself: after all, the cops were after a single man, not a family. Like all addicts, I can be quite the charmer when needed, and chatting the girl up was the perfect cover. My new friend agreed to go for coffee; she even asked if we could meet up again, as we strolled back past the courthouse. I agreed, while thinking to myself, sorry, love, that isn't going to happen.

Once I had made it out of Maidstone, my train journey up to London was straightforward, but my mind was still full of the jailer's terrified face as I held my makeshift weapon to his neck. I needed something to block out the memory and the guilt, so I headed to Plumstead.

So there I was, sitting in the dealer's den making half-hearted small talk in the gloomy early evening. He wasn't looking at me and didn't really seem to care what I was saying. This was about to change.

The TV was on in the corner: the *London Tonight* news programme. The newsreader frowned at the camera and adopted a concerned tone as he read the night's main story:

'Members of the public are warned not to approach a dangerous and possibly armed man who took a security guard hostage before escaping from a Kent court today. Ray Bishop is accused of large-scale people trafficking ...'

I stared at the TV. A well-chosen, unflattering photograph of me at my most unkempt and intimidating filled the screen. I heard a gasp from elsewhere in the room. My dealer host was suddenly paying his guest rather closer attention.

All I could think was that all over London happy families and ordinary people sitting down to eat their tea would be clocking the face of this supposed savage, this public enemy number one. What would they think? Even worse, what would my poor mother think?

Sure, I knew I had done terrible things, but I didn't recognise this monster they were talking about on the telly. I'd never been an evil guy. I'd never wanted to hurt anybody. The child inside me cried out: how had I been turned into this hated outsider?

How had I got here? And what was I going to do?

LONDON CHILD

I suppose people would say that I come from a broken home. There again, I've never tried to blame my upbringing or my difficult childhood for my life of crime and delinquency. That has been all my own work.

I was born on 3 July 1973 in Woolwich, south-east London – later to become synonymous with the cowardly murder of British Army soldier Lee Rigby. I was the fourth of four kids born to Florence McEvoy and Colin Bishop. I can't say for sure, but I would imagine that my dad got pissed to celebrate my arrival, because that was what he did pretty much every day of his life.

My mum always says that I was fearless as a toddler. She reckons that I was a thousand miles an hour and just drove everybody mad every day. When I was very young I went through a phase of demanding to be taken to London Zoo all the time. Mum had to keep a closer rein on me after she caught me trying to climb into the lion's den.

I threw a lot of tantrums and went into fits of rage at the slightest setback. If I were a kid today, I don't doubt that I'd have been diagnosed with ADHD or some such condition. Back then I was just an annoying little bastard.

I've hardly got any memories of my dad at all. All that I can remember is that he used to shout a lot, and once he hit me for drawing on a wall. He spent whatever money he had on booze and never helped my mum with anything.

It must have been a living nightmare for my mum. She had come over from Ireland knowing virtually nobody and here she was, raising four kids and trapped with a moody monster who was no use for anything. It was a lot to cope with and there were times when she just couldn't.

I still have these vivid memories of times when my mum would say she was going to go back to live in Ireland and all us kids would have to go into care. My nan and granddad would take us up to Euston Station to wave her goodbye – but she loved her kids too much and could never do it.

Once it went as far as Mum actually making arrange-ments with social services for them to look after us when she had gone. I would be about four, and I can remember being at Euston, crying and screaming at her, 'Mum! No, don't go!' Once again, she couldn't do it when it came down to it – but those traumatic memories did some major damage to my psyche.

When I was about five, she finally found the courage to sling my dad out. He left without looking back. After that, there were a few times when he would pass me in the street and he would walk past like I wasn't there. The pain hurt like a dagger.

He never spoke to me again. That brief period was the sum total of my relationship with my useless father. It might sound shameful, but when he drank himself to death at fifty I never shed a single tear. He died on my birthday. I felt nothing.

I was closer to my dad's parents than I was to my dad. My nan and granddad on his side were great to me and I loved them because they gave me lots of sweets. Even more than that, I used to love hearing their war stories.

My nan had worked at the Woolwich Arsenal, making ammunitions, and I'd listen open-mouthed as she talked about surviving a direct hit from a V2 rocket during the Blitz that killed a lot of her mates. She also lost both of her brothers during the war: one in Normandy, and one on a beach in Malaysia.

My granddad had been in the RAF and I'd hang on his every word as he told me about dogfights with the Luftwaffe over London. He used to man an ack-ack gun on Shooter's Hill. I asked him so many times if he ever hit any German planes. His answer was always the same: 'Who knows?'

I got on well with my sisters, Caroline and Amanda, but me and my brother Colin fought like cat and dog. Mostly, though, family life was all about my mum. She was a saint who often went without herself in order to make sure we kids got fed and clothed.

Mum did her best but there is no doubt we were a poor family. We never had the snazzy clothes and trainers that most of the other kids did, and having no dad to look after me also made me a pretty easy target. From the age of five I began to get badly bullied.

I don't want to make a big play for anyone's sympathy, because it was just how things were, but my life was miserable for years. Other boys picked on me for my clothes, or for my basin haircut, or for not having a BMX bike. Some kids off a rival nearby estate took the piss non-stop.

I was desperate to be accepted by the other kids but for most of my early childhood I just felt sad and alone. All of the other boys always seemed so much bigger and more confident than me. I was pretty miserable, and often quietly cried myself to sleep at nights. In fact, I did it more nights than not.

In my head, I thought all of my problems were to do with not having a dad. I was so jealous of the kids at school who could go out and do things with their fathers, and I started blaming my shitty life on my dad for abandoning me. I hated him and I didn't know how he could be so cold and unloving towards his son.

After a bit, my mum met another man, Bob, who became my stepdad. It could have helped me but it didn't. By then I hated any kind of authority figure, and if ever Bob tried to discipline me I just fought with him. When he and Mum gave me another sister, Sinead, I just felt resentful and like I was being pushed even further out of the family.

I know, I know, I was a right bundle of fun!

One of the many things that other kids picked on me for was my big sticking-out ears. When I was ten, I told a doctor that I got bullied because of them and the doc explained that it was possible for me to get my ears pinned back through surgery. I agreed: I was so desperate that I would try anything.

I spent two weeks on the plastic surgery unit at the Queen Elizabeth Military Hospital in Woolwich. The operation was fucking horrible and it was incredibly painful but I saw a lot of people in there whose suffering dwarfed mine.

The Falklands War had just finished and a lot of the injured servicemen were in hospital with me. In fact, I used to watch the Chinook helicopters chopper them in over Woolwich. A lot of them had lost limbs and some had been hideously burned when the Argentinians had bombed the *Sir Galahad*. It was horrible to see grown men in such pain and it made me feel like my complaint was just petty and trivial by comparison.

I got friendly in the Queen Elizabeth with a bloke who was in a wheelchair after being badly mutilated when an IRA bomb went off while he was in a military parade in Hyde Park. We had a strange bond because the weird thing was, even at that young age, I had seen the IRA's work at first hand as well.

I had been playing near Woolwich army barracks one day when a huge explosion rent the air. I must have been 300 yards away but the blast knocked me off my feet and I felt as if the air had been sucked out of my lungs. The IRA had blown the gatehouse to pieces, injuring five people and leaving a crater 15 feet deep in front of the barracks.

I'll never forget how terrified I was as I lay there sprawled on the ground, and the bomb certainly didn't make our local family life any easier. It gave rise to even more anti-Irish prejudice than there already was, and as an immigrant from County Galway my mum didn't have a lot of friends.

She always told me that skinheads hated the Irish, and this scared the shit out of me, as there were a lot of them around our way. Too many, in fact. They would go on National Front marches, and once my mum and me walked into a pitched battle on Woolwich High Street with the NF skins throwing bottles at the police behind their riot shields. If I ever saw a skinhead, I ran a mile.

I also steered clear of the local football hooligans who would go on the warpath before Millwall games. A lot of older lads off my estate were in their notorious firm the Bushwhackers, and I would see them outside our local boozer getting pissed up before home games. If Millwall lost and they couldn't get to the away fans, they would usually end up beating up each other.

I thought they were total nutters, and in any case, I was secretly a fan of Millwall's arch rivals, West Ham, after I met Trevor Brooking when he came to some event or other at my school. He had been nice to me – but I certainly didn't walk around south London telling people I was a West Ham fan.

The wider world seemed pretty depressing, really, when I was a kid. It seemed to be a time when one disaster followed another. If it wasn't football violence or strikes, it was the Brixton riots or the King's Cross fire, all of which made a strong impact on my young mind.

Evil seemed to be all around. Even when they caught the Yorkshire Ripper, it turned out that Peter Sutcliffe used to regularly drive his lorry to our neck of the woods to do drop-offs at a factory down the road in Charlton. He would have a couple of pints in a local pub there, the Waterman's Arms.

Of course, all this shit was unfolding against a backdrop of the Cold War and warnings about the nuclear bomb. I would worry endlessly about this, and lie awake in bed wondering if we would really be safe under the dining-room table when a 50,000-degree thermonuclear explosion went off.

Likewise, I spent a while obsessed with the idea that we were all going to drown. Before the Thames Barrier was built we used to all worry about the river's water levels. Every time the test sirens went off, I would be convinced we were all heading for a watery grave.

Looking back, it's amazing to think how crap so many things were in the eighties. Television played a big part in our lives but we only had four channels to watch, which were full of American shows and posh English people who never swore. I never liked *Blue Peter* or *Record Breakers* because the kids on there were such nerds.

Incidentally, another programme I could never stand was *Jim'll Fix It*. The kids on there seemed such losers, and even as a boy I can remember my mum saying that Jimmy Savile wasn't right. Women are good at spotting freaks and weirdos, especially ones who might harm children, and my mum clocked him leering at the girls on *Top of the Flops*, as we called it.

If I watched anything, it would be cartoons or *The A-Team*. My family and everybody else that I knew watched *Only Fools and Horses* but I'm not sure we saw it as a comedy programme. Living on our estate in Woolwich, there were plenty of Del-Boy Trotters around and it seemed more like a fly-on-the-wall documentary.

Like most Irish women, my mum was a devout Catholic and sent me to church from an early age as well as to Catholic primary and secondary schools. Despite this, I could never buy into religion. The teachings all sounded like mumbo-jumbo, and as for the Bible, I just wished it would get to the fucking point. My rational mind struggled to take its fairy stories seriously – and did this 'God' really want to send me to hell every time I looked at a girl's tits or had a wank in the shower?

I found it hard to trust any authority figures, whether they were from the church or elsewhere. I wasn't alone in this. A few of the kids at school were living in council care and they would regularly come in with cuts and bruises given to them by the staff in their home. Once one lad lifted his shirt to show me bruises all over his belly where his carer had stamped on him. Apparently it happened all the time.

When I got to St Paul's Comprehensive School in Abbey Wood, I was quite good at a few things like maths and physics, and I was fascinated by anything to do with outer space, but I played this side of me down in case other kids thought I was a geeky tosser. It meant that school didn't do much for me, although a lot of that was probably my fault.

Even so, after I had my ears pinned back and as I started to approach my teens, the bullying mostly stopped. This was partly because I had started playing the class clown at school and taking the piss out of the teachers, which made me a bit more popular. I suppose if somebody makes you laugh, it is harder to dislike them and hit them.

I had also started doing a bit of boxing at a local youth centre. I liked it because it gave it me more confidence and it meant I didn't feel as weak and inadequate as before. I found hitting a punch bag exciting and exhilarating. I even had a few fights at junior level, but that all came to an end because my coach got pissed off with me for smoking. Well, I was twelve years old at the time.

But the main reason that the bullying stopped was that I got involved with two big gangs around our way: the Woolwich Common Estate Crew and the Barnfield Estate Boys. I was in awe of the bigger kids who ran these gangs on our estates, and would do anything to impress them or to look as streetwise as them.

This often meant getting into fights, which I would happily do as long as I knew I had back-up around me. Because I was so desperate to be accepted, I would go one step further than most of the others, and consequently pretty soon came to be known as a fucking lunatic.

There were plenty of fights with other gangs, although it was all about fists with hardly any knives and certainly no guns around. When I first got involved I'd be scared but I would just throw myself into what was going on with false bravado. I was often the one to throw the first punch.

The first time I ever seriously attacked someone, I was eleven. A fair had come to Woolwich Common, and because all of the local gangs would go, there was often trouble. I was there with a few mates and we saw a kid who had beaten up one of our lads a few days earlier.

We laid into him and I took the lead. We all punched and kicked him to the ground and I laid into him with a dog chain that I used to carry around. We beat him up pretty badly. How did I feel? It was exciting – and I was making up for all those years of fucking bullying.

As I entered my teenage years, my best friend was a guy called Jack Shepherd, whom I had first become mates with at school when we were both about twelve. Jack was from one of Woolwich's biggest and heaviest criminal families and he and I hit it off straight away, seeing each other and hanging out more days than not.

The Shepherds were big news in Woolwich, as were the Arnolds, who were major businessmen who went on to own more than thirty pubs. I looked up to Johnny Arnold, who had worked hard to be an honest businessman. He always tried to steer me in the right direction. A beautiful man. Then there were the Morris family, the Finnegan brothers, Roderick Reid and Steve Clark. In a funny way, they were all local heroes to impressionable kids.

A few of my other teenage mates, like Tommy Eastwood and Lee Brumit, were from gypsy families, and some weekends I would hang out with them at the travellers' camps in Abbey Wood and Thamesmead, sometimes sleeping there.

We would get up to some quite serious shit. One of our favourite activities was nicking mopeds and motorbikes. I learned
to ride them really fast, which stood me in good stead when I
later started my criminal career.

Despite this, I think travellers have a very unfair bad
rep in a lot of people's eyes. Most people that I met on the
travellers' sites were dignified and moral people who were
tough and policed their community well. They were a long
way from the kind of pikeys who will steal anything that's not
screwed down.

A lot of the travellers were Irish, which I could relate to
as I also spent time as a teenager staying with my mum's family in County Galway. My granddad was a lovely man with
an amazing story. He was originally American, and had come
over to Ireland in the 1930s when he had won the New York
state lottery while he was working in Macy's. When the war
broke out he had been unable to get home so he had stayed,
met my nan and settled in Ireland.

The McEvoys were a tough family and were very respected
in Galway. My mum's elder brother, my Uncle Paddy, was
a former All-Ireland champion boxer who in his time had
fought at Croke Park and later became a boxing trainer. He
was renowned and feared throughout Ireland, and even the
travellers that he would sometimes have bare-knuckle prize
fights with were wary of him.

While I was visiting Ireland, I did some more boxing
with Uncle Paddy. He showed me that the mental part of the
sport was the most important of all. I had always loved chess

– although, again, I played that down so as not to appear too brainy and attract attention – and Paddy explained to me that boxing was really just a physical version of chess.

Two of my other Irish uncles, Uncle Kieran and Uncle Mike, also taught me to shoot guns. I would fire at tin cans, as I could not bear to kill animals. Obviously, this talent with firearms was to come in rather useful in my later life.

Back in London, one good mate of mine from school was Nick Love, who has gone on to be a successful film producer who has made great movies like *Football Factory*, *The Business* and *The Sweeney*. I smoked my first-ever joint at Nick's house at about fourteen, was sick as a pig and vowed never to do it again.

Yeah, right!

I had mostly stayed off drugs in my early teens because my mum had warned me against them so convincingly, and two members of our gang had died from sniffing gas. But this abstemiousness ended when I was fifteen and 1988's Summer of Love came along.

The first time I ever took Ecstasy, I felt like I had entered the gates of heaven. My normal edginess, anxiety and anger fell away and I felt total peace and complete love for every-body around me, which was an alien feeling for me, to say the least.

I threw myself into taking E and in no time at all I was living for the weekends. We'd get smashed at the Rave in the Cave in Elephant and Castle on Saturday nights and I'd cadge lifts off older mates to the orbital raves around the M25.

I would get so high on these epic benders that I thought I would never come down.

Of course, I always did. And it was never very pleasant. I also noticed that I seemed to be doing rather more drugs, and getting a lot more fixated on them, than most of my mates. That was definitely a sign of what was to come.

My new narcotic lifestyle was doing nothing for my already rubbish academic career, and at sixteen I left St Paul's comp with three GCSEs and not the first idea what I wanted to do with my life. I drifted into working on market stalls selling jeans on Deptford Market and on Leather Lane in Hatton Garden, and got occasional days' cash-in-hand work as a scaffolder.

Yet I had left school at a shitty time. Margaret Thatcher's Britain was deep in recession and somebody with a council-estate background like mine had virtually no chance of getting a full-time job. I often wonder, in retrospect, just how many sociopaths like me were basically created by that Tory government's ruinous, rubbish inner-city and employment policies.

I probably sound like I am playing the blame game here, but think about it – every needle has a point. Thatcher's Tories never gave a fuck about the young, so obviously we grew up thinking that we didn't have a voice. At least, not unless you talked like you had a plum in your mouth.

Our estates looked like concrete fortresses, with walk-ways blocked off and barbed wire and anti-climbing paint signs everywhere and CCTV cameras beginning to prolif-erate. The official policy of society seemed to be to keep us herded in as if we were no more than animals, so maybe it is no surprise that that is how we started to behave.

The policing on our estate was also disgusting. The local police and the Special Patrol Group (SPG) were essentially badly behaved gangs – just as we were – and operated with their own vicious pack mentality. The only difference was they could do whatever they wanted with the full weight of the law behind them.

The police were often racist, referring to my black mates as 'jungle bunnies' and suchlike, and would fit us up during stop-and-searches for a laugh. I lost count of how many of my mates got arrested after a lump of dope mysteriously appeared in their pockets as the police stopped them at random and frisked them. They wrongly figured that one friend, Paul, was a dealer, and they were always planting stuff on him.

One day they stopped me, happened to see a screwdriver lying on the ground a few feet away, and claimed that they had seen me chuck it there. They arrested me on the spot and charged me with going equipped to steal. I had never even seen the screwdriver before.

With no money and nothing to do, my mates and I would often hang around outside our local shop. One evening an SPG van pulled up and the officers piled out, rounded us up and gave us all a good kicking for nothing. It was a laugh for them, and they knew we could do fuck-all about it. Who were we going to tell – the police?

Alienated, abused and treated like shit, was it any surprise that so many of us frustrated young men inevitably turned to a life of crime? No, it wasn't – and that was exactly what I did.

I did my first armed robbery when I was sixteen. Me and a mate jumped an ice-cream van. We smashed the window with a hammer, then my mate, who was big for his age, grabbed Mr Whippy the ice-cream seller, and held on to him while I jumped in the van and stole about £30 in 20p and 10p pieces and a bag of gobstoppers. I felt powerful. It was great.

Naturally this first taste of crime led to another. One of the first things I got regularly involved with was robbing any delivery vans that came on to our estate. My gang would be on the constant look-out for deliveries of stuff like rental TVs, video players or anything at all we could sell, basically. As soon as we saw our prey, we would pounce.

The poor drivers would not know what had hit them. We would surround the van, smash a window or two and help ourselves to whatever happened to be in the back. We saw any deliveries onto our turf as fair game, and eventually Federal Express and White Arrow declared our estate a no-go zone and refused to deliver there. We also targeted the mail vans.

I felt bad about doing this stuff as my mum had tried to raise me with a strict moral code, but at the same time it was exciting and gave me an adrenaline rush and much-needed money. Mostly, I just went along with the gang that I was still looking to impress.

We stole a lot of cars around Woolwich and the local area. Back then, nicking a car was easy – you would stick a screwdriver in the door barrel, open the door, pull the plastic from under the ignition, snap off the ignition top and start the car with a screwdriver. After a while, I could do it in thirty seconds.

Sometimes we just used the cars for joyriding, and when I took the wheel I'd always want to drive the fastest and take the biggest risks. I was starting to get a reputation as quite a fucking head case, and rightly so. How I didn't kill myself in a stolen motor, God only knows.

We also worked out that if we nicked a car or a van and reversed at speed into the shutters of a local shop, the shutters would just collapse. Then three or four of us would pile into the shop, grab whatever we fancied, and fuck off. Later, of course, this became known as ram raiding.

Looking back, I was a mess, an inadequate teenager over-compensating for his weakness, a psychological basket case, and an abandoned child full of rage at being betrayed by his dad. Barely eighteen years old, I was bitter, immature and confused. So, what was the least rational thing I could go and do?

Yes, that's right. I became a father.

BREAKING DOWN

You couldn't exactly say that Anita and I were love at first sight. After all, I first met her in an adventure playground when we were both nine years old. But we had always got on well, and just after I left school we got together.

By then Anita already had a lovely little girl, Leeanne, and when I moved out of my mum's place to live with them I became her stepfather (her biological dad never bothered with his daughter). In no time at all after I moved in, Anita fell pregnant with our own kid.

It meant that I had only just turned eighteen when Ashley was born. It was exciting being a dad that young but also pretty scary because I hadn't really got a clue what being a father involved. I certainly couldn't take any hints from my own dad, who had not stuck around for long enough to be of any help whatsoever.

I was desperate not to repeat my father's mistakes but the truth was that I was too young, confused, immature, bitter and angry to start playing happy families. It was beyond me. I was drinking and smoking pot, I was still out on the estate getting up to mischief and getting involved in petty crime, and I was giving Anita and me no chance of making it work.

Ashley was only a few months old when his mum and I split and I moved into my own Woolwich council flat. This was the start of a nasty, dark time in my life. Feeling abandoned and unlovable, I began drinking and puffing even more and sank into a deep, self-pitying depression.

I hated being in my flat, where I felt like I was going quietly mad, so I spent all my time getting pissed or high down the local pubs and clubs. I was so aggressive towards anyone who did so much as look at me the wrong way that as often as not the night would end up in a fight. If it didn't, I'd beg to stay the night at mates' houses to avoid being at my gaff on my own.

One night after a few pints I went into a local pub called the Herbert for a few more. The landlord told me he couldn't serve me as he had brought in a new rule that it was over-25s only. He grabbed hold of my shoulder to try to throw me out and I smacked him one and knocked him clean out.

Another time I was playing pool in a pub in Welling and got into an argument with my opponent. He thumped me in the side of the face so I punched him back. The landlord was a right big old unit and he chucked the pair of us out.

We carried on grappling in the street. A bunch of my mates were drinking outside a pub over the road and they all came running over. There was a load of his pals there as well and before long it was pandemonium, like a fucking Wild West scene. The police turned up, nicked everyone they could catch and charged us with Section 18, affray, but the CPS couldn't prove anything and dropped the charges.

One kid I used to know at this time was a black guy, Stephen Lawrence, who was about a year younger than me. I would sometimes bump into him at the end of his street and we'd talk about hip-hop and stuff. He was a nice, quietly spoken guy and nothing to do with any of the gang shit that I was caught up in.

It was a tragedy when Stephen got stabbed and killed by a group of racists who, for all their front, were just a pack of sad wannabe gangsters. A few friends of mine knew them and said they were just a bunch of losers. There were two other racist murders in the area at the same time, but they never got the media attention that Stephen's killing did.

I was still seeing a lot of my mate Jack Shepherd and we would do a little low-level dope dealing together. His family connections meant he could easily get hold of the stuff, and we would sell it around the local pubs and clubs. There was never any shortage of takers.

However, my increasing criminal activities and the brawling in pubs meant that Greenwich police were starting to take even more of a keen interest in me than they were already. My run-ins with them were increasing in number, so it was inevitable that when I was nineteen I got locked up for the first time.

I got given a week's remand in a juvenile centre for stealing a car. It left me fucking fuming as I was totally innocent of this charge: the cops had just picked me at random out of the local bad boys in order to get their crime figures down. I hated being locked away and naturally came out even more hostile and resentful than before.

Looking back, at this point I was a walking disaster waiting to happen. My mood swings had worsened until I would fly off the handle at anybody about anything or nothing. Being off my face all the time wasn't helping, either. My family were really worried about me but I was closed off to them – and to everyone else.

Anita had started seeing another bloke who didn't like me seeing Leeanne and Ashley. One night I bumped into him in Woolwich and slapped him one. His response was to stab me twice in the legs. I still have the scars.

One day I visited my mum and then left to go and see a friend, and suddenly I stopped dead in the street. My legs couldn't move and I felt faint and gripped by fear. I had to turn round and go back to my mum's. Now, I know that I was having a panic attack. Then, I just thought I was going mad.

These panic attacks, or anxiety attacks, kept coming and kept getting worse. I would get a deep sense of impending doom and feel like I couldn't breathe. Eventually, I was so paranoid that everybody had it in for me that I couldn't even leave my cave.

Even within this madness, part of me knew that I couldn't go on like this and I needed help. So eventually I plucked up the courage to leave the flat and go and see a doctor. He realised that I was in the early stages of some kind of serious debilitating mental illness and referred me on to the psychiatric unit at Greenwich District Hospital.

A female shrink, Dr Mounty, assessed me and I rabbited on to her at great length about my fears and problems. I liked her, until she asked me whether I took drugs, which I took severe exception to as I figured, in my messed-up state, that it was none of her business. I distinctly remember thinking: what's that got to do with the price of fish?

I definitely made quite an impression on Dr Mounty, as there and then she sectioned me for twenty-eight days under the Mental Health Act. She diagnosed me with recurring depression and an anxiety disorder and ruled that I could be a danger both to myself and to others. She had definitely got a point.

The hospital gave me two powerful anti-psychotic meds, Stelazine and Haloperidol, and locked me in a padded cell for the whole of my first week. There was a nurse outside my door day and night. My sullen mood was not helped by the Haloperidol giving me a side effect of a locked jaw, which I needed a painful injection in the bum to alleviate.

During that week, I felt as if my whole life was over before it had even begun. One question ran through my mind non-stop: how the fuck did I end up here? I knew that my life was out of control, but I had not expected to end up as the teenage star of a south-east London remake of *One Flew Over the Cuckoo's Nest.*

After my first week ended, I was allowed out of my solitary confinement to mingle with the other patients. This was to prove a decidedly mixed blessing. One of the first blokes to approach me was a man with huge bulging eyes like Garfield the cartoon cat, who shuffled over to me without apparently moving his legs. Speaking through a stutter, he announced that he was one of the doctors on the wards.

This unlikely self-declared medic asked if I wanted a game of pool. When I agreed, he immediately pushed all of the balls into the pockets with his hands and told me that he had won. 'Right you are!' I agreed as I backed away, maintaining eye contact.

Dr Mounty refused to let me go before my twenty-eight days were up so I had no option but to stick it out. I spent the month giving my fellow inmates a wide berth, restricting myself to shuffling back and forth between the coffee machine and the smoking area, and hiding in my room doped up to my eyeballs.

When I was released to live at home with my mum, I was trying to pretend that I was OK but I was not in a good way. I had taken to washing my hands up to 100 times a day, and through my antidepressants and tranquillisers the world was a grey, fearful fog. There seemed to me no way out of my depression and paranoia.

The hospital referred me on to a behavioural psychologist for cognitive therapy. Dr Shah talked to me about my obsessive-compulsive disorders and phobic states and explained to me that one of the problems crippling me was agoraphobia. I told him that I just wanted to be normal, whatever that was. He promised he would help me to manage my symptoms.

I felt lower than ever after my first group therapy session for agoraphobia. Still not out of my teens, I sat in a circle with five neurotic middle-aged housewives as they talked about how they were afraid to leave their houses. The worst thing was, I recognised their stories and the pain on their faces. It was exactly how I felt, as well.

Fuck! I was determined to beat this!

The next six months were a desperate struggle as I strove to escape my living nightmare. I persevered with the cognitive behaviour therapy sessions but each time I dared to leave my mum's house I would be overcome with a crippling panic attack. It would take every fibre of my being to stand still until it passed and not just turn on my heel and run back indoors.

At the end of the six months I was able to get on a bus by myself. As I sat there, I thought I had scaled Everest. While my anxiety was still there in me, for the first time since my breakdown it was manageable. I felt delighted as I reviewed my situation: OK, I was still on psychotropic medication, but I had not had any weed or E since being sectioned.

You know, you have done well here, I told myself. You deserve a celebration. You haven't had a drink in weeks: let's go down the pub and have a few! So I did.

I woke up the next morning in a cell in Woolwich police station.

When the police explained why I was there, I thought they were talking bollocks. They told me I had nicked somebody's car and driven it through the window of a supermarket. The cops said they had found me asleep at the car's wheel.

What the fuck? I didn't have any memory of this at all. In fact, I was convinced that I was being fitted up again, and launched into a disgusted, foul-mouthed anti-police rant. It ended with me being bailed for another court appearance.

The moral of the tale, obviously, is that you shouldn't mix psychotropic medicine with countless pints of lager. And the real irony was that the pub was only five minutes from my mum's house. God knows what I needed a car for in the first place.

I might have overcome my agoraphobia now but I was still a complete psychological mess. I felt like straight society had totally given up on me, and the feeling was mutual. With no feeling or empathy for anybody but myself, I threw myself back into an anarchic life of crime.

A lot of my offences were fuelled by alcohol. I was getting plastered more and more often, and when I was drunk I was getting increasingly aggressive. I was more placid when I was stoned, but I suppose that was also doing its own kind of damage to my fragile mental state.

Some of my crimes were pathetic. Being normally totally skint, I got into the bad habit of shoplifting my groceries. I was not very successful at it, nor very subtle. I would think nothing of filling a supermarket trolley with alcohol and then trying to make a run for it.

Naturally I would often get caught, and it was totally random whether I would try to flee or I would attack the security guard who had pursued me. It was hardly any surprise that I was getting arrested on a regular basis and soon found myself in and out of young offenders' centres.

Often I got nicked when I had not even done anything. Once the police booted down my door, dragged me out of bed and charged me with being involved in a car chase during the night. The fact I had been in bed all night with a girlfriend and we could prove it meant nothing to the cops – or to the magistrates who found me guilty.

The young offenders' centres like Feltham and Rochester were no more than hate factories for young men like me. They all ran on intimidation and fear. Of course, these were emotions that I was well used to, so being thrown in with a load of other self-destructive nutters who hated authority just as much as I did was never going to go well.

On one of my first visits to Rochester I had a fight with the officer on reception as soon as I got in the door. He gave me a pair of shoes that were two sizes too big for me to wear. He knew that if I wore them on the wing I would get mugged off, and that was exactly why he did it.

In prison or young offenders' centres, things like shoes are status symbols. If you had nice clean shiny footwear, it said you were someone. If you turned up in a pair of Coco the clown shoes looking like a cunt, it showed that you hadn't put up a fight at reception and you became a target.

So when the maggot screw gave me the shoes that were too big for me, I refused to wear them. He gave me another pair that were covered in paint and I threw them at his fucking head. We ended up having a scuffle and I was carted off to the segregation unit. Nice way to arrive!

I was so insecure and paranoid that if another inmate passed a comment that I didn't like I would straight away go for him and try to smash his face in. I laid into a black guy, Diamond, who was trying to bully me when we played pool on the wing. He thought he could get away with it because he had his gang around him. He was wrong.

If somebody pissed me off, I would plot revenge. I would sit steaming in my cell and wind myself up, and as soon as they opened the door I would find him and do the cunt. I'd give him a right kicking. Fuck knows how many stupid fights I got into that ended up with the warders piling in to break them up.

That was often when my problems started. Once the screws had broken up the scrap, they were not averse to giving you a good kicking of their own. As they dragged me off to segregation, they would kick and punch me all the way down. A lot of them were ex-Borstal officers and they were right horrible bastards.

When it was a few warders against a problem prisoner such as me, they were rabid dogs. They loved to show just how brutal they were. They even drugged me with an antipsychotic liquid called Chlorpromazine, which was also known as Largactil and was dreaded and notorious in prison circles.

We convicts referred to this delight as the liquid cosh, and we did so with good reason. Once they had pinned you down and injected you with Largactil, it was Goodnight Vienna. There was no way to fight it. You would come to hours later in the segregation unit, having shat and pissed yourself, and you would feel like a zombie for days afterwards. It was barbaric and should never have been allowed. Of course, if you ask the authorities, it never happened.

Once the warders threw me face down on a concrete floor and my head smashed against it with a thud. It concussed me and I was dizzy and had a terrible headache for days. The guards denied me medical care as they knew there was no way they could tell the doctor my injuries were self-inflicted, and they didn't want to get in any shit.

Between the best efforts of Feltham and Rochester, and my own short fuse and mental problems, I was turning into a bit of a savage. As my teens ended the juvenile centres appeared to be my natural habitat and it seemed only a matter of time before I graduated to a full-blown adult jail.

I made it by the time I was twenty.

UNIVERSITY
OF
CRIME

When I wasn't in the juvenile detention centres, my crimes on the outside were getting more and more stupid. I was totally out of control. I would do ridiculous things like get completely pissed then stagger into an off-licence on my estate, pick up two bottles of whisky and lurch out again.

I wouldn't even bother to run. What shopkeeper was going to tackle a nutter like me?

They didn't need to, of course. Their CCTV would record everything, and I was hardly unknown to the local police. It wasn't exactly difficult for them to pick me up, and before long I was back in court on a series of sloppy, cack-handed shop-lifting charges.

There was no point in wasting my time and theirs

pleading not guilty, so I didn't. I was sentenced to six months at Her Majesty's Pleasure at HMP Belmarsh.

Belmarsh was pretty brand new in those days. The rest of London's well-known prisons were macabre old Victorian relics like Pentonville, Wandsworth, Wormwood Scrubs and Brixton. They were notorious as living museums of human suffering where the misery seeped from the walls.

Belmarsh was different. Thatcher's government might have loved public spending cuts but it loved locking up criminals even more, so it had somehow found the money to construct this state-of-the-art incarceration unit. I suppose I should have felt privileged, but I can't say that I did.

When I went into Belmarsh I was bricking it, but naturally I hid that fact behind the mask of don't-give-a-shit, tough-guy bravado that every con wears while they are inside. Once I was settled into the jail's day-to-day routine, it didn't take long for my natural aggression and hatred of authority to surface.

I had been inside for about two weeks when a prison officer pushed me to hurry me up as I was walking through a door on one of the wings. My red mist descended and I clenched my fist, turned round and punched him full in the face.

The alarm bells went off and a whole squad of warders came running across and jumped me, carting me off to solitary confinement and giving me a few good slaps along the way. After a night to contemplate my misbehaviour, during which I felt absolutely fine about it, I was given some news the next morning.

'Pack your stuff!' ordered a gruff voice as my cell door swung open. 'You're leaving!' It was my first experience of the ghost train – what convicts call the sudden departure from one jail to another if you are proving too difficult for the staff in your current prison to handle. It was not to be my last.

I got transferred to HMP Elmley on the Isle of Sheppey, but I was not to last long there either. The screws soon tired of my bad attitude and refusal to do a single thing they told me, and in no time I was back on the ghost train, this time bound for Wormwood Scrubs.

Once I was there they stuck me, not without reason, on C Wing, for prisoners with addiction problems and substance misuse needs, but just as I was getting used to life there they announced they were closing the wing for refurbishment and I had to move on to HMP Oxford. My six-month stint was turning into a whistle-stop tour of the British penal system.

HMP Oxford was one unholy shithole. It looked like a castle, which was no surprise as it had first been used as a prison in 1066 to hold prisoners from the Battle of Hastings. Its last renovation had been in Victorian times. It had actually been condemned as unfit for use in the 1980s, but now had been temporarily reopened to cope with us homeless Scrubs cons.

The place was filthy. I got given a prison job as a cleaner and one of my duties was collecting the metal trays from where they'd been placed on the floor outside the cells after meal times. I soon learned to give them a good kick so the cockroaches would scuttle away from under them before I picked the trays up.

My aggressive attitude continued unabated. One morning at the hotplate in the kitchen another prisoner pushed in front of me to get some food. I told him that I had been waiting before him, and when he told me to fuck off I smashed him over the head with my tray, knocking him out.

There is a rule of prison life: whenever you need something, you can never find a prison officer. A soon as you step out of line, there are millions of the fuckers. The warders that had accompanied us to Oxford from the Scrubs surrounded me as one, giving me the usual kicking en route to segregation.

This was to prove a harrowing experience. The segregation unit at Oxford was the so-called hanging tower, which in the eighteenth century had been the last port of call for prisoners on their way to the gallows that used to stand in the courtyard below. My cell appeared unaltered from those days.

Imagine a dark cobbled cell no more than eight feet square with the kind of dampness that radiates through your bones. There was no window, which meant that it was impossible to read even a large-print book for more than a few minutes. All you could do was sit and stare at the giant medieval walls.

This was to be my home for ten days, twenty-three hours per day. I was let out for half an hour's exercise per day and was given one shower all the time I was there. I had some serious long dark nights of the soul in that hanging tower as my imagination ran riot and I contemplated the terrified condemned men who had spent their last days in that dank space.

I was determined not to let the place beat me, and during the days I gathered my resolve by imagining myself getting my revenge on the warders who had kicked the shit out of me when they transferred me to the tower. Even so, there were points I thought those ten days of solitary would never end.

You might imagine that my first experience of full-blown adult jail was a miserable waste of time with no redeeming features. On the contrary – I was to learn things and meet people in there that were to stand me in good stead for the whole of my criminal career.

I had gone into Belmarsh scared, confused and basically not sure how to live, having been starved of male role models to that point in my life. However, as I toured the South-East's nicks for the next six months, I found plenty to admire.

The prison system is like a university of crime, and I was a keen student. There was no shortage of veteran career criminals willing to share their thoughts and philosophies, and as a man seeking direction I looked up to them.

Unlike me, they commanded respect. They had something about them.

It may sound stupid, but for the first time in my life I felt like I was being educated. I was being given some direction. They seemed like wise, savvy men who shared my mindset and my circumstances, but who knew what they were all about. They had an identity. I longed to be like them.

So I learned what I guess you would call, for want of a better phrase, the old-school London criminal code. It was pretty simple:

- You never ever talk to police, and you never steal from your own.
- You respect your elders.
- You never do scummy things like burgle people's houses.
- You never hurt women or children.
- You hate all grasses and sex cases, and if you get a chance to do them harm, you take it.
- You stay away from junkies because you can't trust them (but booze and weed are OK).

Like the impressionable soul that I was, I absorbed all of this information and adopted it as my mantra, my moral code, for years. What a place to form your philosophy on life! Deep down, I think I vaguely sensed that I might be taking a wrong turn, but so what? For once, I felt like I belonged. It was an exciting feeling.

After four months in the medieval hell of HMP Oxford, I was given my civvy clothes back and £43 to help me start a new life. As I walked through the streets of that cathedral city, I was struck by how picturesque and beautiful Oxford was. It seemed clean and fresh. Naturally, I got straight on a train and headed back to the dirty, grotty London I knew.

So what did I do now? I was desperate to stay out of trouble and not go back inside. This didn't mean I was going to keep my nose clean: far from it.

I knew now I was set on a life of crime. But this time I was determined not to get caught.

A condition of my release was that I had to attend probation, which I dutifully did. Old-school probation officers were a great bunch of characters, and the Irish guy I was assigned was no exception. He was almost as big a fuckwit as me.

Paddy – let's call him Paddy – sent me to attend an alcohol awareness group and lectured me at length about the evils of the demon drink. He didn't seem to see any contradiction between this and taking me for a couple of pints after our probation sessions. Paddy would then head home to his wife and family, and I would stay in the pub and get roundly pissed.

Was I an alcoholic then? I suppose I was but I never thought of myself like that. I knew that my dad was an alcoholic and I hated him so I didn't want to be anything that he was. In any case, I thought that alcoholics were the tramps and sad cases that you saw sleeping on park benches, and I knew that I wasn't like that.

I was an enthusiastic drinker but not a very good one. I still lost the plot very quickly when I drank and got into a lot of fights. Often I didn't even remember the fight the next day, when I woke up covered in cuts and bruises. As well as that I was doing a lot of drink driving, which wasn't really a very good idea.

No, drinking was not really agreeing with me, and I needed to find another high to replace it. Boy, was I about to find it …

THE DEVIL'S DUST

I'll never forget the first time I snorted a line of cocaine. I was in a pub in Woolwich with my best mate Jack Shepherd, who produced a small wrap of white powder and asked if I fancied a line. I was so pissed that I could only just manage to slur 'yes'. We went to the toilet, he passed me a rolled-up £20 note and I sniffed the lot. Nothing seemed to happen. We returned to the bar.

Ka-boom! It hit me like a grenade.

Everything in the pub had changed. The barmaid was a lot more attractive than she was before I went to the toilet, and she was definitely the girl I was going to settle down and have my next kids with. The intimidating meatheads at the pool table were suddenly mere mice, as in my mind I was now far mightier than Rambo.

As soon as I opened my mouth, I also discovered I had developed the superpower of baffling people with my bullshit. For the first time in my life, I could talk seductively to attractive girls. I could feel my chest swelling. I had arrived, and my God was I going to let the world know it! My inner chains snapped with an almighty clang and the beast in me was released.

On the way home, my Ford Capri seemed to have changed into a supercar of sorts. My perception of the world had altered forever as Jack and I spent the rest of the night snorting and planning our world domination. Everything out there was ours for the taking, and nothing could possibly go wrong, right?

At this point, I was still doing a little bit of scaffolding work. In between my spells inside, I was drifting around different scaffold firms learning the trade. In my experience, most scaffolders have at least one screw loose, so I fitted in very nicely. They are a unique breed: never pick a fight with one if you can avoid it. But scaffolders' wages couldn't support my brand-new coke habit, so I drifted deeper and deeper into the world of crime.

From mere shoplifting, I quickly graduated to commercial burglary. High streets in those days were not the CCTV-lined minefield they are today. It wasn't long before my mates and I came to regard all shops as targets, and we would regularly smash windows or drive stolen cars through their shutters to steal our bounty. Then we'd meet up with one of London's many fences to exchange our loot for money – or, as we saw it, cocaine tokens.

Our favourite targets were the big electrical stores and fashion houses. Nobody would ever have mistaken my slap-happy crew for slick professional thieves, but we were game as fuck. We would regularly play cat and mouse with the Metropolitan Police, and high-speed police chases became a regular adventure.

We would often target Marks & Spencer because they had a habit of leaving large floats in their tills overnight. They used to have small windows in their store doors, and if you jammed a screwdriver in the side of them they would fall right out. It was a piece of piss.

Marks & Sparks also used to have a lot of sale goods hanging from the ceiling, and you didn't have to be Einstein to work out that they were blocking the infrared sensors. We knew that if we stayed low to the floor we wouldn't set the sensors off, so we would crawl on our hands and knees to the till areas.

We would lever the till open with the screwdriver – pop! – grab the £500 or so that was in there, then go on to the next one. It could not have been easier. Some of the big M&S shops had a fleet of twenty tills, so the rewards for our nights' work were pretty fucking substantial, to say the least. We'd leg it out of there with £15,000 or £20,000.

We would also take books and books of gift vouchers, which were as good as cash. Marks treated them like normal money at the time, so if you walked into one of their stores with a £20 voucher and bought a 99p sandwich, they would give you £19 in change. We did a lot of that.

Another favourite target was Tandy, the electrical store. They were so fucking easy and we did them so many times that, between you and me, I sometimes wonder if it was us that put them out of business.

Tandy had many flaws and one of them was that their security system was pretty unsophisticated. It was simple to pull a shop's alarm off the outside wall, run up the road with it going off in your hand, stamp on it and then dump it. That was the alarm disabled.

We would then hide out and wait for an hour or so. Some of the alarms didn't go through to the local police station, so if the cops didn't show up after a while we'd know we were safe to go back in and burgle it. The shop was ours to do what we liked with. It was like being a kid in a fucking sweet shop.

Some stores' security was connected to the local cop shop, and what we would do then was to wobble a screwdriver in the door to set the alarm off deliberately, then run away and hide. The police would turn up, find nothing amiss and call the store's key-holder to come out and turn the alarm off.

As soon as the key-holder had re-set the alarm we would do the same thing again, and the police and the key-holder would have to repeat the whole rigmarole. Naturally by now the key-holder would be pretty pissed off and would figure there was a fault in the alarm and leave it switched off. *Voilà!* Once again, the shop was ours for the taking.

The beauty of Tandy was that they sold radio scanners. They cost around £1,200 even then and they were invaluable in the underworld because you could use them to listen to the police radios. We would flog them for £400 or £500 each. In no time we were supplying half of the London underworld.

All of these scanners would naturally immediately be tuned in to the police frequencies. We knew exactly what they were. I had a list of all the local police station frequencies – Woolwich was 17410 – that I had been supplied with by a local bent copper.

Once you had those frequencies, you would listen in to the police radios as you did a job to see if they were onto you or they were in the area and it was all going to come on top. The scanners were like gold dust and, thanks to Tandy, we had a lot of them. Our fences couldn't get enough.

Some people who weren't even involved in crime would buy the scanners to listen to the police radios for entertainment. I would often be in a pub in Woolwich and some bloke would say to me, 'Oh, I had the police radio on last night, I heard your name.' I'd laugh: 'Oh yeah, what did they say?' It all helped us stay one step ahead of the police.

The cops knew we were on to them and it pissed them off. It was an offence to listen to police radio so if we ever got caught we'd hit the scramble button to change the frequency and then play the idiot. But the police knew what we were doing and would always confiscate them.

We were playing cat and mouse with the police all the time. They would regularly raid my place, normally at about five in the morning. They would burst in mob-handed and turn the place over. They knew I wasn't stupid enough to leave anything incriminating there – it was their way of showing they were on to me.

At the same time, there was a weird mutual respect there. I might go to a club in Woolwich and turn around to find four or five coppers standing there that I knew and who regularly raided me. We would have a laugh and a joke and even buy each other a few drinks.

I even had one detective constable in one of those clubs tell me, after a few drinks: 'Ray, I love you!'

'Why's that?' I asked, surprised.

'Because you give me so much fucking overtime,' he replied.

'Don't worry,' I told him. 'I'll be giving you plenty more.'

Once the police had a surveillance car, a Vauxhall Cavalier, parked outside my flat. It stood out a mile, not least because all of the police cars had sequential number plates, which in Woolwich was UYL. They weren't exactly hard to spot.

The car was there for a few days, and one night a mate and I spotted it empty and nicked it. We just took it and went joyriding and then hid the car in an underground garage. The cop had nipped to the local shop and left it untended.

He got in all sorts of grief because he had left his scanner, his warrant card and all sorts of papers in there. The next time I got raided, which was pretty soon after, the officer was on the team and sat me down for a quiet chat.

'Look,' he told me. 'Do me the favour of getting me back that warrant card and that scanner and we'll say no more about it and I'll owe you one.'

He winked at me, hopefully.

'Well,' I told him, 'I don't know nothing about it, but I'll see what I can do.'

Shortly after that he got an anonymous tip-off by phone that he might want to have a look in the underground car park. He did – and I think it might have saved his neck. It was the same car park the police always suspected that I was storing hooky gear in. As it happened, they were absolutely right.

That copper didn't forget it, because a few weeks later he gave me a pull in Woolwich when there was a warrant out for my arrest. I hadn't turned up for a court appearance. By rights, he should have nicked me there and then, banged me up overnight and taken me to court in the morning.

'You know there's a warrant out for your arrest?' he asked me.

'Yeah.'

'Well,' he said, 'get yourself down the magistrates' court in the morning and hand yourself in. It'll look good for you and we won't object to you getting bail.' I did, and he did exactly what he promised. You scratch my back …

At the same time, that kind of beat-bobby policing was dying out. There was a new young brigade of pricks coming in who just wanted to make a name for themselves. People like the SPG were brutal, horrible bastards. Those were the fuckers who caused the Brixton riots to kick off.

Another of my sidelines was stealing cars for villains to use as getaway vehicles. A few of the more notorious south-east London armed robbers would give me a few hundred quid and tell me where they wanted the car to be left, and I would do the rest. Then later I would hear about the heist on the news.

I needed to do these jobs to feed my growing habit. Me and my mates were always gasping for cocaine, and we would go on nightly benders that normally ended up at Paul Allen's house in Woolwich Dockyard or at Jack's flat in Thamesmead. Paul was a formidable cage fighter and could fight like fuck.

Incidentally, Paul was later to be jailed along with another friend of mine, Lee Murray, for masterminding Britain's largest-ever cash robbery. They relieved a Securitas depot in Tunbridge Wells of £53 million. Had I not been detained in a maximum-security jail at the time, I would almost certainly have been on that job myself.

We were a connected young crew, and back then you needed to be in order to get cocaine. It was not like today, where it seems readily available to everyone. You really had to know a man who knew a man who knew a man. Thankfully, we did.

Quite a few of them, in fact.

Jack Shepherd was growing into a very successful cannabis dealer and I'd regularly help him out. We had one setback when Jack bought 30 kilos of puff with a street value of about £60,000 from a heavy gangster in Bermondsey. We gave it to a guy who was doing some couriering for us and he promptly vanished with it.

This looked pretty bad and we knew the Bermondsey villain would come after us, so we devised a plan. We knew the disappearing courier's brother, and invited him for a night out. At the end of it, we pulled a gun on him, took him back to Jack's flat and held him hostage.

We didn't hurt him; we let him sit and watch TV while we left menacing messages on his brother's phone. He was with us for two days before his terrified brother finally showed up and gave us what was rightfully ours – and some hefty compensation on top.

At the same time as Jack and me were doing stuff like that, we were also trying to be decent dads. Jack had a couple of young kids about the same age as Leeanne and Ashley, and we would take them on joint days out to places like London Zoo or Thorpe Park. It's weird: morally we were a mess, but we were doing our best by our kids.

As my coke addiction quickly grew more severe, though, my crimes grew more spectacular. The drug was driving me mad and I seemed to be living in a state of permanent rage and frustration. Every day I would need a few drinks just to take the edge off my paranoia. At times I felt like screaming.

I took to buying and dealing guns. Many south London firms had ready access to them, as after the Gulf War and Bosnian conflicts many of the guns seemed to make their way on to our streets. I once bought a Kalashnikov AK-47 with a fully activated firing pin from a Gulf veteran. It had been brought back deactivated as a trophy by a young soldier. The firing pin was then reinserted in the UK. I had no intention of using it for crime; it just fascinated me.

You could literally buy these things at boot sales, as it was not illegal to own one as long as it was deactivated. It was not difficult to convert it to being fully operational again. Starter pistols like the Brock could also be easily converted to fire live .38 rounds. Many of the other large guns such as the Uzi that appeared on our streets had been reactivated in this way.

Bullets were also a lot easier to smuggle and there were people who dealt solely in ammunition. It was not illegal to own bullet casings by themselves – just think of those belts that you can buy that have casings as a fashion statement – so certain people would buy them and then insert the explosive charge themselves in garden-shed factories.

I spent a lot of my time going over to Essex and staying with a traveller mate, Philby, in Fobbing near Basildon. Behind his gaff there was a large field with disused vehicles in it, including a battered, abandoned old coach. It was a right ugly-looking thing, and in my permanently paranoid state it used to give me the creeps.

One day I decided to use it for a spot of target practice and lined up some cans at its windows. As a kid, I used to shoot at cans with an air gun for kicks, and I thought it would be funny to do the same thing with my Kalashnikov. With a couple of friends, I emptied my machine gun of all its magazines and didn't hit a single can – although the armour-piercing bullets did riddle holes right through the coach.

A dog walker found some shell casings, saw the bullet holes along the coach and told the police. It created a panic, as it was obvious that a high-powered weapon was involved. My fingerprints were on one of the casings so I got arrested a week later. They couldn't prove I had done it, so after search-ing my house and finding no gun they left me alone.

Yet after this I seemed to get arrested by armed police more and more. I got rid of the AK-47 as I had used all the bullets and couldn't get any more, so it was now useless. Even underworld ammunition dealers didn't have a lot of call for armour-piercing and high-velocity rounds. Mind you, you can probably buy them at Tesco nowadays.

Anyone who has ever held a firearm will tell you the same thing I found. It gives you a strange sense of power and invin-cibility. In a flash you go from being a semi-rational human being to a potential killing machine. At the wrong time in my life, I could have created absolute carnage with a weapon like that. Luckily, the worst that I ever did was to use them as instruments of fear.

With three friends, I committed a series of armed rob-beries to fund our narcotics-fuelled lifestyles. We called our-selves the Team. Looking back, we were unbalanced individu-als without a clue, and initially many of our robberies were bungled and amateurish. But we learned as we went along, and gradually we became good at what we did. In fact, we became very good.

So who were the Team? (I have changed the names here, but only slightly.) Danny was a mountain of a man who always seemed totally calm and collected in even the most dangerous situation. His presence alone could strike fear into anyone. Pete and Chris were totally fearless in executing our schemes. I became a meticulous planner who obsessed over every detail. We were a formidable unit – and over an eighteen-month period, we became prolific.

We had all grown up together on the estates and in school. That was important, that we all knew each other inside out and trusted each other implicitly. The biggest danger in any criminal enterprise is infiltration, but there was no danger of that – and we knew if one of us got caught we would hold our water and not grass the others up.

The Team's favourite targets were jewellery stores, and places with ready access to cash such as banks and bureaux de change. We'd carry out an advance observation of our intended target and plan the best way to hit it. Every member of the gang would have an assigned role, with the emphasis always on speed and efficiency.

We could hold up premises and be back in our getaway vehicle in less than two minutes. By the time people had even begun to comprehend what had taken place we were gone. The element of surprise combined with speed made us incredibly effective.

Let me give you some idea of what it was like to commit an armed robbery.

On arrival at the intended target, you become acutely aware of everything around you. You notice every car and person in your line of sight, and assess all possible threats to your plans. Your mind is racing uncontrollably as fear and adrenaline dictate your every move. Every passing face looks like that of a familiar police officer and you do constant double takes on everyone.

You notice everything in your peripheral vision with great clarity. You look at each member of your team, and the communication is done in silence. There is no need for words as all that needs to be said is done with the eyes.

A nod from each member seals it as you venture beyond the point of no return. Game on! As you enter the target, all sound is muffled, as all that you can hear is your heart, beating loud in your ears.

Chris always stayed with the getaway car. When the rest of us were in the building, we assumed our pre-assigned roles. Big Dan's job was to man the door to prevent anyone leaving. Pete and I issued the commands and got the bounty. I was a natural at this: I loved the power of being in charge, and I was pretty good at looking and sounding menacing.

Being the bad guys, we had the advantage of being the only ones aware of what was about to happen. We were mentally prepared for it. The unfortunate victims were not – and only found out the grim truth as our weapons were revealed for the first time.

'Nobody fucking move, this is a robbery! Do as you are told and no one will get hurt!'

Time would freeze for what seemed an eternity. Your mind took a snapshot of the looks of horror and shock on everyone's faces. We made a point of letting them see that we were armed, but we did not point our guns at anyone. It was amateur and unnecessary to do this. People tend to freeze with a gun pointed in their face, and it would make the next phase of compliance harder.

Depending on how many people were there, you would either order them to lie on the floor or herd them together. I would then watch over them as Pete grabbed the cash or the jewels. When he had got the prize, he would nod at me and it was time to make our exit.

It was here that we all composed ourselves again. If the police were going to ambush us, this would be the time, so it was important to stay calm. It is not like the movies, where thieves exit a robbery with all guns blazing and screeching tyres – quite the contrary. People outside the building were oblivious to what had just taken place, and the last thing we wanted to do was draw attention to ourselves. Why on earth would you create any more witnesses than necessary?

The last person to leave was always Dan, who had manned the door through the operation. We would all get in the car and pull away calmly so as to not attract any attention. Then it would hit us with an almighty slam. Real time caught up with you again: what had just seemed to last an eternity had in fact taken no longer than it takes to make a cup of tea.

We would usually have a second vehicle parked less than a mile away and quickly change over. Often we torched the first one to destroy any forensic evidence. We would drive back towards the scene, as the police would be looking for people heading away from the crime.

We would then split up so we were no longer a gang of four men. Pete and I would get a train home as we both looked quite nondescript with our glasses on. As a matter of fact, we made a point of looking a right pair of nerds. It worked: no one ever gave us a second glance.

We also broadened out from armed robbery to committing a series of smash-and-grab raids on jewellery shops. For these, we would use high-powered motorbikes instead of cars. It made getaways a whole lot easier as alleyways and pavements opened up for us.

We grew in confidence, and our crimes became more audacious. On one occasion we attacked a jeweller's window in broad daylight with a fireman's axe, stealing the diamond rings on display. These we sold for a fraction of their real worth. When the money was spent, we were off and running again.

Sometimes we just drove vehicles into shop windows. My talent was spotting weaknesses in stores' security. Once I worked out that we could steal an expensive item by reversing a lorry with a scaffold pole sticking out of its back through a shop window. All we had to do was to make a big enough hole to get an arm through.

Bizarrely, soon after I had this idea but before we had done it, another team used the very same technique on a jeweller's shop and stole a priceless diamond necklace. It was a weird coincidence.

Eventually we moved away from using motorbikes. The catalyst was the death of a dear friend, Mark, who decided to ride his Honda 1150 CBX to pick up his girlfriend at the end of a night's heavy drinking, although we all told him not to.

The police later claimed they saw him riding erratically and chased him: Mark died, along with his girlfriend who was a passenger, when he hit a lamppost in Eltham at 127 mph. I had also crashed a few weeks earlier. We thought that we were the dog's bollocks on our bikes, but the truth was that we were dicing with death. It seemed that, no matter how recklessly we behaved at this time, we thought we were untouchable.

A CELL OF MY OWN

Given our increasing recklessness, it's no surprise that our raids began to get ever more ambitious. We even committed one robbery inside the so-called ring of steel. The police had set up a series of armed checkpoints throughout central London after the IRA had detonated two massive bombs in the City. It would have been a serious deterrent to most gangs, but in the midst of our coke-fuelled mania we thought we were invincible.

A girl who worked in a boutique near Cannon Street told me that there was going to be a big lump sum of takings in the shop's safe. The first job in hand was getting hold of a getaway car, but luckily that was a speciality of mine.

We decided to steal a London taxi. We nicked it from outside Paddington Station. I did that more than once: it was weird how many cabbies would leave their engines running and their keys in the ignition when they popped out for a piss or to get themselves a cuppa.

The boutique bird had tipped us off that the best time to do it would be just around six in the evening, just before the shop shut, but the Team got up to London around three. To kill the time, we naturally decided to spend the afternoon in the pub and ended up getting half-pissed.

We were all in zip-up black bomber jackets but underneath them we were wearing suits and ties to help us merge in and make our getaway afterwards. The robbery went OK, but right at the end the shop manager panicked and went running off into a back room.

I shouted at him, 'Where the fuck are you going?' but then he reappeared with wads and wads of loose notes. Our bags were full and we had nowhere to put it so I just stuffed the money into my elasticated bomber jacket and zipped it up again. It's the kind of stupid fucking decision that you make when you are half-pissed.

After the boutique, we went into the William Shakespeare pub next to Cannon Street. The plan was to dump the bomber jackets, then stroll, suited and booted, to the station, where our getaway man was waiting for us in the taxi.

The pub was packed with businessmen and stockbrokers, enjoying an after-work pint. Without thinking, I unzipped my jacket and – whoosh! About £25,000 or £30,000 in loose notes went flying all over the floor around us.

Everybody in the pub was staring at me in stunned

surprise and the only thing my pissed brain could think of to do was to shout, 'Don't worry, it's just the takings from my shop! Has anyone got a bag, please?' It was farcical, and not quite the kind of low-profile, anonymous exit we had intended to make.

Somehow we got out of there, made it to the taxi, got out of the ring of steel and crossed the river back and forth before heading down to Bermondsey and torching the car and the jackets in some disused garages just off Spa Road. We had got away with it, but I fucking shat myself for two or three years expecting a knock on the door for that one.

At the same time, we thought we were untouchable. We plotted ever more daring jobs, including an audacious plan to rob the Queen's House in Greenwich. One room housed the jewels, and the corridors there were so wide that I figured I could ride in on a 600cc motorbike with a shotgun-wielding accomplice on the back, and do the place in minutes. We didn't do that job in the end, but it was a close thing.

There is no doubt the police knew what we were up to. One post office in my home area got robbed three times in a month; the local train station got robbed twice; a betting shop got done four times. They strongly suspected we were behind them, but had no evidence.

The raids on our homes continued on a regular basis, but we were careful and they never found anything to tie us to the robberies. They would sometimes pull me in on a minor misdemeanour to give them a chance to question me. I never gave nothing away. I got arrested for possession of a box of shotgun cartridges they found in the underground garage, but without any fingerprints they couldn't pin them on me.

I was leading a charmed life and it felt to me like I would never get caught. Yet I was so emotionally numb that I would agree to do stupid shit. Somebody offered me five grand to do a contract killing on a gangland figure. By then, it was well known that I was a nutcase and that I had access to heavy-duty firearms.

I can hardly believe it now, but I agreed to do it. Thank fuck the guy changed his mind and it never happened.

Of course, every criminal slips up eventually, and naturally I was no exception. The mistake that was to put me away came on a raid on a Marks & Spencer store in Bromley.

Somebody who worked in the shop had tipped me off to the job. You get people like him – they're not actually criminals themselves but they hang out in the pubs and like to drink with the faces, so they have a drink or two and let slip a few tit-bits of information.

He said there was about £30,000 in gift vouchers in a grey safe in the corner of the shop manager's office. Originally, the plan was for an accomplice and me to do the store while it was still open, and to point a gun at the manager while he opened the safe.

We decided that was too risky and so used our tried-and-trusted method of breaking in at night and doing the tills. We also managed to get the safe open, so we got away with £57,000 in cash and gift tokens.

I had worn gloves, as usual, but they were plastic latex

ones, and when I cut my finger on the broken glass in the door as we broke in, it left a fingerprint through the plastic. I also left enough blood for them to get DNA evidence – just when DNA testing was revolutionising policing.

I was up in court on two charges – the Marks & Sparks job, and stealing £420,000 in tax discs from the main post office in Bromley. The police had nicked two of my mates not far from the scene of that particular crime and had caught me a mile further away. They had no forensic evidence on me for the post office job and no witnesses, but I was charged with conspiracy and got found guilty by association because I was a known associate of the other two and we had previous form together.

On the Marks job, though, I was bang to rights. With the DNA evidence, my barrister said I had no chance of getting off, as it was a billion-to-one chance that it wasn't my blood. I pleaded guilty and got three years nine months. I got two years concurrent for burglary of the post office.

Actually, it was probably a good time to retire from the scene. There had been a pandemic of armed robberies in central London in recent months, and in response the Home Office introduced what seemed to us tantamount to an unofficial shoot-to-kill policy.

The police had formed a unit known as PT17, which was known in the underworld as the execution squad. If ever a case went to court they would always insist they shouted warnings before they opened fire, but the chances were that if PT17 caught you on a job and you had a gun in your hands, then they shot first and asked questions later (if you were still alive, that was).

PT17 had killed two men from my area while they were robbing a security van. A third member, Ollie, survived with a bullet lodged near his spine. Now, I was not there and do not know who opened fire first, but Ollie told me afterwards that the police opened fire with no warning, at least any warning that he heard. Not long after, the same unit shot dead another robber in Woolwich and seriously injured his accomplice.

Around the same time, a senior copper at Woolwich police station that I got on OK with pulled me to one side. He was blunt in his warning: 'Ray, if we catch you doing a bit of work, we have been instructed to kill.'

Between you and me, it's the kind of warning that you tend to remember. Maybe I was better off in the nick.

Funnily enough, I can still clearly remember how I felt as I entered the gates of High Down Prison in Surrey. My main emotion was relief. I knew a force inside me was out of control and propelling me closer to insanity. I wasn't just a danger to society – I needed saving from myself, and instinctively I knew it. I just didn't know what to do about it.

High Down had just opened and I was to be reunited with many of my fellow fuckwits from previous jail sentences. Although I was desperate to reform, I felt compelled to give the warders shit. At times, I would be friendly; at others, disruptive and difficult. I went into the jail's treatment pro-grammes for drug problems and anger management, but also puffed cannabis every day and wound up the warders.

They would take my wind-ups very personally. After an inmate had escaped from another jail, I made a rope ladder out of my sheets and hung it from my window just to take the piss. They immediately got the hump and carted me off to segregation. That's the problem with the prison authorities: no sense of humour.

Actually, there were a whole load of problems with the prison authorities at High Down. One of the main ones was that a certain number of the screws were nasty, sadistic, revengeful bastards.

One of their favourite tricks was called 'Control & Restraint'. If you kicked off, a gang of them would grip your hands behind your back and force your chin upwards so it restricted your airways. It meant if you struggled, it was hard to breathe.

When they had you in C&R they would march you along, and if you fell, as cons often did, they would sit on your back until you 'calmed down'. There was a real danger of asphyxiation – if you struggled they would say you were resisting them, but you were just trying to breathe.

The screws also loved tripping you up in C&R as you were going down the metal stairs to the segregation unit. That was a big favourite at Wandsworth nick. There again, that worked both ways – I managed to send a warder flying arse-over-tit down the stairs by 'accidentally' flexing my arm while we were cuffed. He was off work for two weeks.

I know for a fact that prison officers have killed inmates using C&R, and a good mate of mine still wears a colostomy bag because of injuries he got through it. Not that you'll ever read about that in the *Sun* or the *Daily Mail* – it's all about how prisoners live pampered lives of luxury. Yeah, right.

I was always tooled up in jail for protection, as were most other inmates, and when the warders did a search of my cell in segregation they found a knife that I had hidden under the sink. Naturally I claimed I knew nothing about it and it must have been there when I moved in, but it pissed them off and they were looking for revenge.

This wasn't the only thing I did that antagonised them. I played chess a lot on the wing at High Down and hardly ever got beaten. I just have the sort of strategic brain that is able to think sixteen moves ahead – it has always been my curse and my blessing. My reputation reached the ears of one of the warders, and he challenged me to a game.

We played three games and I won all of them. He didn't like this and clearly thought I was taking the piss, because shortly after the third game, as I was lying on my bed in my cell, he came in with three other screws and they beat the shit out of me during a supposed random cell search.

I put up a fight but I couldn't do much against four of them. However, I fucking held it against him and brooded on it for a few days. Then I came down for breakfast one morning and found him on duty supervising the inmates.

Pretending I hadn't noticed him, I mooched around picking up cornflakes, milk, sugar and toast, then wandered over to him. I suddenly shouted his name, and as he swivelled round to look at me I hit him with my cornflakes like a custard pie.

It was fucking hilarious, and it is a sign of how unpopular he was in the jail that most of the other screws were laughing along with the cons. I didn't even have any comeback for that one. There again, I suppose I was on segregation already!

Segregation at High Down was an oppressive unit, manned by many ex-Wandsworth and Brixton officers. Opposite me was little Dave Goddard, who had been the first man since Ronnie Biggs to escape from Wandsworth. Some other prisoners had tried and failed by hijacking a JCB while they were on exercise, but Dave had managed to scale the wall while building work was going on.

Also in segregation was the notorious Charles Bronson. I got on well with Charlie and he loved me, partly because we had a common interest in boxing, but mainly because he liked my attitude towards the screws and the fact that I never backed down. Contrary to the general misconception of him, Charlie is not a psycho. He has just fought the system for years, and the system is not without fault. He has been treated very badly by screws trying to make a name for themselves.

Charlie is a fantastic artist as well as an accomplished writer. I've kept in touch with him, and when he heard that I was writing this book he drew me a picture and wrote at the bottom of it, 'Box it smart, Ray, you done good, I'm proud of you.' I hope Charlie is released one day, where I am sure he will go on to do great things.

My mum would bring Leeanne and Ashley in to see me. I used to love their visits and would look forward to giving my kids a hug and hearing all their news. Yet again, though, the warders took the piss just because they could.

Visiting was supposed to be from two to four, but the screws would deliberately take so long to process the visitors that you wouldn't get to see them until well after three. They treated them as if they were criminals, as well. It caused a lot of tension – and a riot in one prison, Whitemoor in Cambridgeshire.

After two months in segregation in High Down, I got transferred back to HMP Elmley on the Isle of Sheppey. I got on well with my fellow prisoners there and I even quietened down towards the screws, who just seemed to want a quiet life. I met some sensible lads, and I was, as always, drawn to my fellow Londoners. I puffed whenever I could and by now I had also taken to abusing psychotropic medication.

I didn't even know what I was taking half of the time, but as long as it numbed my emotions I didn't care. I couldn't afford to be fussy as the drug that I really craved – cocaine – was not available, so I had to make do. I went to the gym and saw physical fitness as a way of passing the time and being mentally strong.

Eventually I was transferred to Aldington Prison in Ashford, Kent, to complete my sentence. With just six months left to serve, I was determined to knuckle down and get on with it. I was missing Leeanne and Ashley – he was now three – and I desperately wanted to be the dad that I never had.

So I told myself that this was it for me: on release I would stay away from drugs and crime. I even believed my own bullshit for a while, but it was never going to happen. I was still too steeped in criminal thinking.

As a Cat C prison, Aldington was a lot less secure than the Cat B Elmley. Originally built to house prisoners in the Second World War, the blocks were decrepit, in need of repair and not remotely burglar proof. With other cons, I burgled the prison canteen and hospital, stealing all the available drugs. They could not prove who it was as half the jail was stoned, so we all got away with it.

Incidentally, this period also saw the nationwide out-break of mad cow disease. Prisoners of this country have never been treated to so much beef. For a while our diet featured beef stews, steaks, burgers, griddles and hotpots. I swear we even had beef-flavoured cornflakes at breakfast.

A lot of inmates at Aldington were serving time for importation offences. I met many smugglers who had been nicked at either Dover or Folkestone ports and listened to their stories and boastings of rich rewards with deep interest. It became my new mission to get as many contacts in this world as I could.

It was a free educational crash course in a form of criminality beyond my expertise – and, once again, I was to prove an eager student.

NOTHING TO DECLARE

Despite my occasional outbursts of bad attitude towards the warders, I had largely kept my head down during my prison sentence for the Marks job, and it paid off. I was released after fifteen months of my two-and-a-half-year sentence and re-emerged into the world in better mental and physical shape than I had left it.

I had about £100 to my name and felt that I deserved – and definitely needed – rather more. My head was full of dreams and fantasies of extreme wealth and luxury, and if I had learned one thing in my life so far, it was that crime was the best way of attaining them. In fact, given the sorry state of my CV, for me it was probably the only way.

To me, London seemed to have changed during my fifteen

months away. It seemed edgier and more violent. To my dismay, several friends and associates of mine had been killed or scarred for life in various disputes during my unwanted absence from the scene. One mate, Darrell, had been stabbed to death outside the Plough & Harrow in Welling, a regular drinking hole for me.

Another pal, Terry, had the top of his ear torn off in a fight over a coke deal. Being the lunatic that he was, Terry allegedly avenged this by tracking down his assailant and shooting him four times with a .22 pistol. One of the bullets missed his heart by a few millimetres. Somehow the guy survived, but he wisely took it as his cue to exit the local scene.

One tragedy was particularly barbaric. An associate of mine – let's call him Vic – had got into a dispute over a drug deal gone wrong while I was inside. Vic was not a violent man, and whatever he did wrong he did not deserve the terrible retribution that was wreaked upon him.

Vic was taking his kids to a fireworks display. He had just put them in the back of his car when a man appeared from behind some nearby bushes. The guy shot him six times at point-blank range. When the police arrived, his kids were trying desperately to wake up his lifeless body.

The word in the underworld was that Vic had been accused of stealing money from a cocaine baron. He had protested his innocence, but to no avail. Nobody was ever arrested for the murder. It was symptomatic of the times and just how ruthless and cold-blooded criminals were becoming.

Cocaine was becoming a pandemic and the people moving and dealing it were utterly heartless. The serious money that coke barons were making excited the jealousy of rival gangs. There were more guns on the streets – and they were getting used a lot more. Coke was making people so psychotic that human life meant nothing to them.

Another difference that I clocked was the huge increase in black-on-black crime and shootings. The Jamaican Yardies controlled the crack cocaine trade in Camberwell and Brixton and their ruthlessness brought a whole new level of menace to the criminal underworld.

Make no mistake; the Yardies struck fear into the hearts of even established organised London firms. This new breed of hungry, uneducated thugs didn't care about reputations – and they would kill anybody for peanuts.

By then I had met quite a few Jamaican gangsters in prison. They were often pretty mental characters, and unless Bob Marley was there to translate, you had no hope of following their patois. The truth was that a lot of their disputes had actually begun on the streets of Kingston before being played out in Britain.

I was often amazed inside to meet a Yardie who was even younger than me and discover that he was already serving a life sentence for multiple murders. Most of them were oddly stoical about their sorry plight and just seemed to accept it as their lot. Their attitude was bred in the gutters of Jamaica.

The problem was that this cutthroat culture was adopted by a lot of the disaffected young black English kids. The arrival of Yardies and their values into already impoverished black communities turned them into a powder keg. Yardies and local hoods fought vicious battles over the lucrative crack trade on a continual basis.

Now, I may not be a social scientist but I know a bit about being an impressionable young man desperately trying to climb out of the gutter. Those black kids were even more fucked than I was. The colour of their skins meant they had even less chance of securing a job and a future and they felt even more disenfranchised.

In this anarchic world, gun battles became so common that the news often didn't even bother to report them. Just after I got out, there was a pitched gun battle between two gangs in broad daylight right in the middle of my estate. The police later claimed that one of the weapons used had been a Mach 10 sub-machine pistol.

The police response to this lawlessness was to send armed patrols to parts of south London and set up Operation Trident to tackle black-on-black crime. I didn't envy them their task.

For my part, I hooked up again with old associates and was up and running in no time. Luckily, the drugs trade still had opportunities for go-getters like me. I made regular trips to Rotherhithe to pick up cannabis which my crew and I then distributed through Woolwich and surrounding areas.

Another run saw me collecting coke from Greenwich and, with my pal Danny, selling it through a network of dealers in the pubs and clubs of south London. Danny and I were making a shitload of money, and this – combined with the arrogance born of regularly snorting our wares – made us think that we were the dog's bollocks.

We were frequently at war with rival gangs in the pubs that we were operating in. The cocaine trade was so lucrative that it was no surprise people were trying to muscle in. It was commonplace for gangs from neighbouring boroughs to come and try it on in Woolwich to test us out. We couldn't look weak. It would be the kiss of death.

One night I got into a fight with a bloke from a rival crew. Three of them jumped me and stabbed me in the arm and legs. My wounds would soon heal but my pride was hurt, and I plotted revenge on the fuckers furiously.

I knew the pub they used as their base, and a few days later, when they were all in there, someone went and fired a CS gas canister through their windows. A friend of mine had bought it while he was in South Africa and managed to bring it back with him through customs. It was the first attack of this kind in the UK and made the national news. It was also seriously bad for the business of the pub, which had no choice but to close down.

Another time we let a rival firm know that we were not to be fucked with by firing shots at a snooker hall where they hung out and blowing two of its windows out. The automatic shotgun I had procured from some of the East Europeans on our estate was perfect for this mission. I got on well with them and they could supply me with anything I wanted, including high explosives. I didn't know much about these weapons, but I was keen to learn so that we could car-bomb rivals.

I found myself fascinated by guns and acquired so many that I could probably have started my own war. For a while

I acted as a middleman in transactions between an Albanian Serb that I knew called Ali and local criminals.

I sold Derringer .22 pistols for £250 each and a snub-nose .38 revolver with a silencer for £800. For myself, I bought a Glock .9mm which took sixteen bullets in a magazine and one extra in the chamber when cocked. This set me back £1,200. I stored it in a safe house for protection, should the need ever arise.

One danger of the gang lifestyle was that we were supposed to stick together if anyone had grief. We were still pretty young – I was twenty-four – and fucking stupid, so rows were always kicking off over women. Some members of our firm were total liabilities in this department, and God knows how often we had face-offs and confrontations with rivals over totally stupid things.

This chaotic behaviour meant we were always firmly on the radar of the authorities. We knew the police had us under constant surveillance in the pub that we used as our base. However, we controlled the publican as he was absolutely petrified of us and so turned a blind eye to our many activities.

The cops were using an office over the road from the pub as their observation point. A cleaner who worked there tipped us off. My sixth sense told me that they were planning a raid, so my crew fucked off on an impromptu holiday to Tenerife. The next day, the police raided the pub mob-handed, hoping to nab us with our drug stash, and were frustrated to draw a blank.

The Tenerife trip brought its own dramas. After falling asleep on the beach and burning lobster-red, I could hardly move and so spent most of the jaunt drinking and plotting in a bar called Rah Rah's owned by a geezer called Tony Palmer.

Tony, also known as Big Foot, was from the Broadwater Farm estate in Tottenham but had moved out to Spain after the 1985 riot that saw the murder of PC Keith Blakelock. He had also done amateur boxing with me and even made the British amateur squad, and had made a good life for himself on Tenerife.

Tony looked after me while I was on the island, including helping to spirit me away after I had lost my rag and chinned a local taxi driver who had tried to rip us off. I owed Big Foot for that, and was really upset when he died of a heart attack a few years later.

Back in London, I made an important decision. The heat from the police was just too intense in Woolwich and our operation was too chaotic to last much longer. It was only a matter of time before we all got arrested – most likely for something stupid – and I resolved to get out while the going was good.

I got back in touch with a mate called Mick, whom I had met in Aldington jail. Mick had an international operation going and was doing very well for himself, and I wanted in. He gave me a position in his business, and the next week I was off to France.

My first job was to meet a courier from Holland to pick up a consignment of cocaine. The coke arrived vacuum-sealed in Belgian biscuit boxes to thwart police sniffer dogs. I was then to go and book into an F1 hotel in Calais and await further instructions.

Mick got in touch and sent me to the Cité Europe hypermarket to meet a courier who was playing the part of a day-tripper and had arrived in a coach party. I slipped him the coke and he successfully spirited it back to Britain through the unsuspecting customs. This was a very efficient system and we repeated it plenty of times. Even if customs had found the parcel on the coach, how could they prove who it belonged to?

We also made use of European football matches to hide packages of coke on supporters' coaches. The thinking here was obvious: what sane customs man would want to take on searching and interrogating a bus full of pissed-up English football fans? They would always get waved through, and many a consignment of firearms, stun guns or CS gas made it into Britain by this route.

Nevertheless, I knew that I was vulnerable and potentially at risk in this new job. If I got caught carrying around a load of drugs, it would mean a long spell in a French jail. Knowing this, I was ultra-careful in all I did and always made triple-sure that I was not being followed anywhere.

I memorised the local public transport system and used it a lot so I would never get lost and stand out. I even tried to look French by mimicking the locals' dress sense, which didn't involve a beret and onions around my neck but did go as far as a jumper with a French flag on it.

Over the following year, my activities took me backwards and forwards to the continent many times. We always used the same tried-and-trusted method but the merchandise varied. It was usually cocaine or cannabis, but I also found myself diversifying into smuggling firearms.

The first time I did this, I collected a bag from a courier from Holland and immediately sussed that it was far too heavy to be drugs. Back in the sanctuary of my F1 hotel, I opened it up to be greeted by the sight of six handguns and a load of ammunition. This threw me a bit, but I stuck to the script and did exactly what was expected of me.

We were good, and I was proud of the fact that we rarely lost a parcel. Most seizures are intelligence-led and I was working with a team who knew how to keep their mouths shut. Consequently, the money kept coming in thick and fast.

My lifestyle was pretty debauched, to say the least. By now I was drinking pretty hard and spending a lot of my down time in London casinos. I hardly went near the gaming tables – instead, I would sit spending two grand a night on the one-armed bandits. I would win the jackpot two or three times in a night and just shovel it back in.

My own coke habit was also by now assuming fairly epic proportions. I was sniffing three or four grams of pure cocaine every day. My mind was constantly racing, my heart was pounding and I was sleeping less and less as I spent piles of money as freely as I earned it. I was taking coke just to function normally and couldn't begin to imagine life without it.

Mentally, I was as fucked up as ever. Part of me felt that I had arrived and was finally worth something as a successful international drug smuggler. Inside, though, I felt like a total fraud. At heart, I felt like somebody with a hole in their soul.

Our business got slightly derailed for a while by a shortage of good-grade cocaine. As part of their war on drugs, the American authorities hit on the ingenious idea of placing strict controls on the exportation of ether to Colombia. They knew this chemical was of paramount importance in the distillation of cocaine.

The Colombian cartels were having to use other chemicals instead, and it seriously affected the quality of their product. By the time it got to Europe the coke was often yellow, stank like petrol, caused nosebleeds and rotted away users' septums. When I saw the notorious photos of Daniella Westbrook off *EastEnders*, I knew that there was somebody who had been sniffing some seriously inferior goods.

While our prime product was temporarily off the market, my firm took to smuggling cannabis instead. This was to mean my relocation to the southern Spanish town of Fuengirola. This town was slap bang on one of the loveliest Costa del Sol beaches and so was a bit of a tourist trap.

We needed to transport larger quantities of dope to the UK to make it worth our while, so the only feasible method of transport was lorries. It became my job to oversee the collection of goods in Cadiz and arrange their transportation on to Alicante, where they would be loaded onto a UK-bound vehicle.

I was called on twice a month to do this and had various means of getting the cannabis up to Alicante. My favourite was to pack the tyres of a car with packages and then phone a local vehicle recovery company. I would claim that the car had broken down and needed to be towed to nearby Valencia. I could then follow at a safe distance and make sure the car was not under surveillance before I collected it and dropped it off where it needed to go.

Nevertheless I knew I could not afford to be complacent and I changed my methods regularly. Sometimes I would make use of unsuspecting couriers and delivery companies. After I had set up an address for the goods to be delivered to, I could let them unwittingly take all the risks for me.

Let me give you an example. Once I bought five cheap old washing machines from a second-hand shop and had them delivered to a workshop in Mijas that a friend rented out to do motor repairs. I stashed 35 kilos of cannabis in the bottom of each machine and paid a transport company to deliver them to a storage address in Alicante.

Once the machines were safely delivered, I left it a few days and then went and picked them up in a van and paid the storage depot. I then put the cannabis into three large sports bags that I delivered to a prearranged spot in Valencia.

From there, my cohort would load the stash onto a lorry that was delivering car parts to Ford in Dagenham. The Ford driver was bent and in on the operation, and because the company was so reputable customs would virtually always wave his lorry through. He would then do a drop-off in the UK before delivering his legit cargo to Ford.

My life in Spain was hectic but we also had a good laugh. I would spend a lot of my downtime at my friend Del's villa in Puerto Banús. His place overlooked the site of the filming of the rubbish BBC soap opera *Eldorado*, and we would often have a beer and watch the flimsy plotlines unfolding before us. I can't say I was surprised when it was taken off.

I also hung out with a bloke called Rocky. He was actually on bail for manslaughter at the time – he was working as a doorman in Tenerife and had allegedly killed somebody. To me, he was just a nice guy to chill out with.

The night times were rather busier and more high-risk and dramatic. My Puerto Banús friend had the task of overseeing the collection of cannabis from our friends and suppliers in Morocco. This would arrive on phantom speedboats straight from Tangiers.

Under the cover of darkness, we would sit in a van with a pair of binoculars watching the Gibraltar Straits for any patrolling police boats. When the coast was clear we would send up a flare, and within twenty minutes we would hear the distinctive hum of a speedboat engine approaching in the distance.

Action stations!

My heart would be beating like crazy as we waited to meet the boat on a beach near to Banús. The only thing on our minds was to load up and get out of there fast. We would drop the contraband in a garage in a place called Calahonda, from where it was vacuum-sealed and taken to the transport point.

At this point I had given up puffing dope, and while I was snorting like crazy, on the whole I was pretty efficient. This was what I was in Spain for. Every drop was an adrenaline kick for me, not least because I knew that each successful operation was worth at least ten grand to me.

I got friendly with the Moroccans that we dealt with. It may sound silly given that they were international drug smugglers but they were really good guys. They always produced the goods for us, and the situation was that their product was worth virtually nothing in their country so they were grateful for the business.

The Moroccans regularly tried to give me upwards of a ton on the strap. The biggest load that I ever carried was 150 kilos. Any more than this would have been too difficult to transport onwards. My bosses also figured that this was the most they could afford to lose if an operation went wrong.

Things got frustrating for us when the Spanish coastguards tried to crack down on narcotics smuggling and took to patrolling the waters far more diligently. They would send up helicopters whenever they spotted a phantom, which meant that many a valuable load got slung overboard. We were even up against Royal Navy frigates patrolling off Gibraltar.

I was good at the job but on my nights off I was a typical Brit abroad. I decided that I didn't much care for the Spanish and would get pissed and start petty rows with waiters or bar staff. These arguments turned physical far more often than was sensible.

One night a barman smashed a Budweiser bottle over my head for no more reason than that I was English. I couldn't do much as he had five mates with him, but the next night I returned mob-handed to find them. They weren't there, so I heaved a bar stool through the window as we left.

I also got into run-ins with the authorities. A scar above

my left eyebrow is the result of an encounter with the Guardia Civil when I was driving on the nearby motorway one day. A policeman pulled me over as he said I had a dirty number plate. I was drunk, but he was just looking for a bribe to let me go – their usual routine.

He made the mistake of insulting me for being English and I informed him that he was a Spanish prick. The policeman pulled out his Glock revolver and pistol-whipped me before sending me on my way. I finished up in hospital having six stitches.

It was the last straw for me and I knew it was time for my Spanish adventure to come to an end. Despite the fantastic weather and the money I was making, I was missing my kids and mates and I was missing England. It was time to return to London.

I took a lot of cash back with me but it didn't last too long. I fell back in with my old crew who were all still raving sniff heads and were delighted to learn that I was newly minted. Suddenly I was Mr Popular, subsidising everybody else's coke habits and spending stupid money on benders in casinos. One night I lost six grand on the roulette table. The truth was, I hardly knew how to play.

Meanwhile I continued to find myself in constant trouble. I did a drug deal with a Dutch firm to import some dope but they stitched us up and a parcel went missing. I knew where one of their blokes was based in Aylesford in Kent, and went round there one night with a shotgun and fired two cartridges through his window.

Needless to say, there were repercussions. A few nights later I was in the Ship pub in Plumstead. I came out, jumped into my car and went to pull away. I didn't even see the geezer who fired the gun at me, but suddenly the car's entire window was a pile of broken glass.

Generally, though, I was beginning to see there was no future in importing. Customs had tightened up their borders and improved their detection methods. It was getting far harder to make money by smuggling, so I just went on spending it instead. I rented a beautiful flat in Sidcup, but hated being on my own there so only went home if I was with a woman.

Otherwise, I just crashed in hotels. It may sound stupid, but I think I was doing this because all of the activity around me reminded me in a subconscious way of being in prison. It was the only place that I really felt safe and at home.

The coke was wreaking havoc on my equilibrium and mentally I was not well again. I would dread waking up in the night and would gobble sleeping tablets to try to stop it happening. When I did wake up, I got the fear good and proper.

With smuggling a diminishing option, I considered going back to my old game of armed robbery. Thankfully, for once, sanity prevailed. The SO19 and PT17 flying squads were still coming down on villains like a ton of bricks and the courts were dishing out draconian sentences for even minor robberies. Even I could see it was a mug's game.

Even at my criminal peak I have never been a mastermind or a gangster. I am an opportunist, and my opportunities were becoming few and far between. The feeling descended that I had nothing to offer the world, and I began to loathe myself.

Returning to my roots, I went back to being a drug dealer. But I was no longer a master of my trade – or myself. My addiction had got so bad that I would buy a load of coke and then just snort it myself. By now I could easily get through an ounce of Charlie, with a street value of about a grand, in just over two days.

Suddenly, rather than being Mr Moneybags, I was falling into debt and people were getting notably reluctant to lend me money or bail me out. I knew I couldn't go on the way I was, and I needed something to change before I went mad.

Before too long, the change arrived. Guess what? As usual for me, it involved going back to prison.

SHIP AHOY!

CHAPTER 7

It was Christmas of 1998, Britain lay covered under a thick layer of festive snow, and a friend of mine, Danny J, and I had come up with a blinding idea. We had decided that we were going to rob an amusement arcade in Medway in Kent.

This decision was an excellent illustration of two defining themes of my criminal career at that point. Powered by a potent combination of cocaine and desperation, I found that I was getting increasingly reckless in my disregard for the danger of getting caught. It was almost like I didn't care any more. My misadventures were also getting more random – but there again, as I say, I've always been an opportunist.

In fairness, there was a degree of logic in our choice of this particular target. An associate had told us that the gaming machines had not been emptied over the entire holiday period and so would most likely contain well over fifty grand.

Danny and I settled on the small hours of New Year's Day as the best time for our intrepid heist. We figured that policing levels would be low as the cops would be distracted looking after New Year's revellers. It was probably the last rational decision we made on the entire caper.

Having immobilised the alarm system by stuffing the bell box with expandable foam, we snuck into the arcade with two large holdalls. What we had failed to take into account, however, was just how heavy many thousands of pounds are when they are made up entirely of coins.

We had hardly begun to scratch the surface of the money that was there for the taking and already our sports bags were full and getting very hard to carry. We held a quick Mensa committee meeting and decided the best idea would be to unload the coins into our Vauxhall Senator and come back for more. We didn't really see that we had any choice.

Struggling back out of the window with our deadweights of £1, 50p and 20p coins, we were spotted by a security guard who was looking after a nearby building. Danny and I had no idea that he had seen us, and were back in the arcade emptying the slots again when suddenly a torch shone into my face.

The torchlight was coming through our open window. Two faces were outside peering in: a policeman and a fucking massive Alsatian. The cop yelled at us: 'Come out now or we will send the dogs in!'

We hardly had a chance to comply with this order because the dog was in the window and at us before we could blink. Now, I am generally an animal lover, but I make an exception for police dogs. I have a history with Alsatians, and it is not good.

My right leg bears a permanent four-inch scar from an altercation with one of those furry fuckers in my younger days. I had been hiding in a hedge after a car chase when it found me and fastened its teeth around me. When they have a hold on you, it is game over. They never let go.

Police Alsatians always seem to have a sneering attitude. I swear that when they capture you they always seem to smile at you. As this one bounded towards us, I think it even shook its head at our stupidity. I didn't blame him.

It's a golden rule of criminality that when you are nicked you always deny everything, even if you are caught red-handed. I felt a proper mug doing it on this job. Snow had been falling since we had started the job, so a lovely clear set of our footprints led from the building straight to the back of the Senator.

Here we go again! Danny and I were remanded in custody and carted off back to Elmley Prison on Sheppey. This place was starting to feel like a home from home. I recognised a lot of faces, among both my fellow cons and the officers.

Prison is like that. After you have done a few sentences, everybody seems to merge into one. My reputation as being trouble and attacking staff can precede me and cause me grief, but on this occasion the warders treated Danny and me fairly and we had no cause for complaint. The same went for our trip to Maidstone Crown Court, where we both got eighteen months.

Three months into my sentence I was on my travels again, this time back to another old stamping ground, Belmarsh. This time I was facing a potentially more serious charge: grievous bodily harm and issuing threats to kill under Section 18.

This trouble had arisen when my boy, Ashley, who was by then seven, came to me in tears because a geezer had yelled at him for playing near his house and had confiscated his football.

The man who had done this was a notorious local bully so I had gone round his house to have a word with him and get Ashley's ball back. When he opened the door he swore and took a swing at me, so it seemed only right to return this greeting with interest.

Our fight had taken place in the hallway of the guy's house but nevertheless the Crown Prosecution Service had somehow assembled a cast of witnesses of good character who had seen the entire fracas. It didn't look as though I stood a chance in court. My defending QC, who was a genius named John Higgins, thought differently.

A brilliant Queen's Counsel in full flight is a marvellous thing, like watching a champion boxer or a chess grandmaster at the top of their game. Mr Higgins made verbal mincemeat of the guy who was supposedly my innocent victim, and soon had him raging and swearing in the witness box.

This thug's hot-headed temper tantrum played right into our argument that he had been the aggressor and I had only hit him in self-defence. I think that my favourite bit of the cross-examination (and he certainly was cross) came when Mr Higgins gently scolded him ('Now, now, temper, temper!') and offered him a glass of water to calm him down.

In my experience, juries get things right more often than not and it didn't take this one long to find me not guilty on all charges (not words that I often heard!). Relieved, I returned to Belmarsh to see out the rest of my sentence.

If you can have such a thing as a favourite jail, Belmarsh is probably mine. Unlike a lot of other lock-ups, the staff seem to have a certain respect towards their prisoners, even – or maybe especially – high-security regular inmates such as me. I've never come to major grief in there, which is a rarity.

During this particular stay, I was working hard towards self-improvement. I had volunteered to go on the drug-free wing – the wing for prisoners with previous addictions and drug histories who want to go straight, and so sign up for random voluntary drug tests.

A lot of inmates have no interest in staying clean and only go on the wing to work their ticket, or because it looks good on parole reports and sentencing plans. My participation was genuine. I was not a happy person and I was at least shrewd enough to know that a lot of this unhappiness was down to my prodigious drug intake in the past.

In my halting, instinctive way, I was making some progress towards sorting myself out. I was even entertaining thoughts of trying to get some sort of education when I got out. But I am a man who lapses easily, and a horrible setback was to push me back towards my personal abyss.

The death of my best friend Jack Shepherd hit me hard. My mum broke the news when she came to visit me with my kids. She told me as gently as she could but it was still a hammer blow: 'Jack's gone.' It seemed he had been having a little party at home on his own one evening and he had died of a heart attack and brain haemorrhage. He was the same age as me: twenty-seven.

I had always felt like Jack was one of the few people who got me and really understood me. He had always tried to look out for me. The last time I had seen him I had been out of my head on a mad one, and Jack had looked sad and worried and asked me to get some help.

I had promised him that I would. Of course, I never did – and now he was gone.

A priest called Father Kevin held a beautiful memorial service for Jack in the prison chapel the following Sunday. My friend Mark Epstein, another cage fighter from London, and I both did readings and we all prayed for Jack. All of the old-school London chaps like Charlie Kray were in attendance. A few weeks earlier, I had attended a service in the same place for Charlie's son, Gary, who had also died young.

I liked Charlie and thought it was ridiculous that he was serving a twelve-year stretch at his age after being found guilty of plotting to import £39 million worth of cocaine into Britain. The evidence against him was laughable and he claimed that the police had fitted him up. It was obvious to everybody that he had been sentenced harshly because of his surname.

Despite that, Charlie never moaned about his plight and

he always conducted himself like a true old-school gentle-man. Even so, getting a sentence like that in his early seventies slaughtered him and he deteriorated more and more before my eyes. Inside two years, he was dead.

After Jack's memorial, I slunk back to my cell, sat alone and pondered my lot. I felt hollow and desolate, and no mat-ter how hard I tried I could not see a way out of my depres-sion and sense of worthlessness. My life seemed empty and I couldn't see how I could make it better.

Despite my mum being a staunch Catholic, I had never had any time for religion and maintained the arch scepticism I had felt towards it ever since having it rammed down my throat at school. Now, though, I felt like I needed some help and guidance. I went back to Father Kevin and asked to make a confession to him.

Father Kevin was a good man and heard me out. I told him of my many faults and self-loathing and he assured me that God would forgive me for the life I had lived to that point. His kind words touched me. I guess I normally heard so few.

I can't claim that I converted to a good and godly life right at that point but I did feel as though God had entered my heart in some way. I seemed to become more aware of the beauty in the world and more able to appreciate things like birds in a summer sky, or a rainbow. Sadly, though, I still had plenty more chaos to come in my life.

I saw out the end of my sentence for the slot arcade job in a very unusual location. Due to overcrowding in the British prison system, the government had decided that they would temporarily house some convicts on a ship. This sounded like a change and great fun to me and so I happily agreed to serve out my last few weeks on the ocean wave.

I was transferred from Belmarsh to HMP Weare in Portland Harbour in Dorset, and on the way down my head was full of visions of both *Captain Pugwash* and a majestic *QEII*-style ocean liner. When I got there, however, I was to be severely disappointed.

HMP Weare was an ugly floating monstrosity. It looked like a series of shipping containers bolted together and painted rain-cloud grey, but less glamorous than that. The poor Dorset local yokels must have been mortified to have this scrapheap and a load of crims dumped on their doorstep. I doubt it made it on to too many of the tourist postcards.

HMP Weare had quite a chequered history. It had originally been built in Sweden as accommodation for offshore oil and gas industry workers before being sold to the UK to house soldiers during the Falklands War. I spoke to one of the prison officers there who had actually served during the conflict. The government had then sold it as scrap and it had ended up as the rehab wing of Riker's Island jail in New York.

Britain had now paid millions to buy it back and it had been towed back home from its mooring place off the coast of Manhattan. Quite how the old rust bucket had made it all the way across the Atlantic was a mystery to me. It didn't look like it would have passed any nautical MOT.

The ship had five landings and they put me on the fourth, which was the drug-free wing of this particular jail. I was still deadly serious about my attempt at rehabilitation and applied for an onboard drug-awareness programme known as the Alchemy Project.

When I was accepted, I found that I considered myself to be different and possibly superior to my peers on the course, who were mostly heroin addicts. I had the London criminal's code engrained in me, which told me that junkies were sad cases and not to be trusted or taken seriously.

The counsellors introduced me to the twelve-step programme. The first time they told me about it, I thought it was a total load of bollocks. I had always had a problem with God, and when they said I had to surrender control to 'a higher power', I just thought, 'Oh fuck!' Even if you didn't call it God, it seemed like it was pseudo-God to me.

Nevertheless, I focused on the programme and learned a lot about addiction. Despite this, my engagement with the process was purely intellectual. I couldn't begin to let down my hard street image and discuss my delicate inner feelings, and so was nowhere near the humility that you need to overcome addiction.

In fact there was a strange paradox about my behaviour at this time. I felt few real feelings except for anger and sadness, and when my depression was at its most intense I would over-compensate with black humour and banter. Thus I was probably at my funniest when I was the most down.

I will never forget one moment on HMP Weare when I felt as if I was transcending my miserable circumstances and self. On 11 August 1999 there was a total eclipse of the sun, and as the black descended the normally noisy ship fell silent. As the moon fully blocked the sun and cast its shadow across the earth, I actually felt free and a part of the world.

The next month I was once again released from the prison system, but this time I was on a mission. I was to continue my drug and life rehab on dry land and away from London. I was eschewing crime and putting my future into the hands of caring counsellors and medical professionals.

I set out for a new life by the seaside, of all places. But instead of the fresh start I craved I was to plunge into a pit of addiction and despair. It was time to use my special talent again and once more pull defeat from the jaws of victory.

FROM SEASIDE TO SMACK CITY

To a man like me reared in the graffiti-strewn rat runs and concrete jungle of south-east London, Bournemouth looked impossibly scenic and picturesque. Could this chocolate-box pretty Dorset coastal town really be my new home? The air seemed clean and fresh, the women looked glowing and gorgeous and the golden beaches stretched for miles. I fell in love with this earthly Paradise.

The reason for my relocation was that I had procured some funding from the probation service to do a spell of residential rehabilitation for my ongoing struggles with coke and booze. I was to stay at a centre called Quinton House run by a woman called Lorraine Parry, who had been an addiction expert for more than thirty years.

Rehab is a slow and gradual process but naturally I wanted to go at it at a thousand miles an hour. On my first day at Quinton House, I stormed into the office and demanded to be given some step work to do. I can still remember the exact words that the senior counsellor, Tony Riley, said as he looked me up and down on that sunny day: 'Somebody get this fucking lunatic to the beach!'

Tony was laughing hysterically as he said it and clearly bore me no malice at all, but the encounter was indicative of just how mental and unhinged I was at the time. I was to find out later that some people referred to me as the Tasmanian Devil. Even when sober I seemed to have a screw loose.

My manic nature was exacerbated by the fact that I had just come out of the prison system, where everything is regimented and proceeds at a slow, methodical pace. I had spent so long in the nick that I was in danger of being institutionalised, and when I did get outside, where everything moved far quicker, I would over-compensate by moving at hyper-speed.

I had zero attention span and was an obsessive multi-tasker. I would regularly find myself cooking, ironing and running a bath all at once. Nagging away at me constantly was the fear of missing out on something. I was later to learn that these were all classic traits of the addict mind.

Lorraine Parry told me a little about myself and why coke was my drug of choice. She said it suited my personality. In general, addicts of stimulants like cocaine tend to be quite extrovert and manic, while people who turn to opiates such as heroin are more introverted.

I was very much in the first camp, a natural risk-taker who liked being the centre of attention and could be selfish and egocentric. People like me tend to be obsessive-compulsive and impulsive, and so we often place ourselves in dangerous situations. Rubbish at relationships, we take emotional hostages instead, often being controlling and manipulative.

Lorraine went on to explain that my character type can often be seen in quite high achievers and deep thinkers. Nevertheless we are prone to anxiety and breakdowns as well as depressive illnesses and psychosis. We expect high standards in ourselves and others, and are blaming and resentful when they are not met.

Problems arise as we are unreliable and unmanageable without chaos in our lives, and so we create stress artificially in order to function effectively. Thus we tend to operate like coiled springs and are susceptible to emotional outbursts and irrational thoughts. We are rarely happy or satisfied and we can be emotionally illiterate, unable to distinguish a feeling from a thought.

Lorraine concluded by saying that, at worst, my personality type was prone to being grandiose and narcissistic and, at times, incredibly violent. It was hard to disagree with a word she said. This woman was reading me like a book.

I am clearly a very extreme example of this character type. Over the years, psychiatrists and psychologists have often diagnosed me as bi-polar or manically depressed. Obviously, as an addict I also swing between poles as I am either up or down without drugs.

When I went into Quinton House I had already been clean of drugs for three months. Nevertheless, Lorraine warned me that I would find it difficult to recover. She said my over-analytical mind would probably be a handicap rather than a help as I fought to kick my addictions. Put simply, I was too clever for my own good.

The best example of this very perceptive point is that my mind was so busy racing ahead and trying to figure out how I could solve the problem myself that I didn't really listen to Lorraine properly or take in what she was saying. She explained that my drug use was just a symptom of a much deeper condition. However, while I understood that my previous anxiety attacks and agoraphobia were forms of obsession, I failed to make any connection with my substance abuse.

I just figured that I was special; I could cope. As long as I didn't use, I would be OK.

Recovering addicts often latch onto another obsession to replace drugs or alcohol, and I soon found mine. Quinton House residents were allowed to go to the gym three times per week. I started going with a few of them, and in no time at all I was hooked.

I found that lifting weights and building muscles gave me a sense of power, and I felt good the more I went. I would leave the gym on a high and thinking that I couldn't wait to go again. I would be sitting in discussion and therapy groups at Quinton House, but rather than paying attention I would fantasise about my next trip to the gym.

My three permitted gym sessions a week weren't enough,

so regardless of the rules I started going four times a week, then five and then six. I pumped iron like I was training for the Olympics and knocked hell out of a punchbag, as well as taking up running. My torso was getting so developed that I looked like the Sugar Puffs Honey Monster. I thought that I was easily beating the drugs. Actually, I was turning into even more of a fucking nutcase than I already was.

I looked physically intimidating now, but inside I was still so emotionally fragile that it was impossible to connect with anybody meaningfully. Nevertheless, I figured that it would help me if I had a proper girlfriend again.

Addicts are strongly warned against forming relation-ships with people in the same treatment groups as they gener-ally lead to dysfunctional relationships. Sick plus sick equals sick, as the saying goes. Naturally I decided that this did not apply to me. An attractive Irish girl staying at Quinton House called Sharon caught my eye and I decided she was the one.

It took me no time to decide that I was head over heels in love with Sharon and we would set up home together. We would take fantastic holidays, live in the country and have lots of kids and grandchildren. It's hard to tell if she felt the same, as this conversation was all taking place in my head.

Even so, Sharon and I spent a lot of time together over the next few weeks and did become a couple. True to my manic nature, I was trying to do her recovery for her as I was by now convinced that I was absolutely fine and didn't need any help at all, especially as I was now getting on for eight months clean.

My treatment now became all about her, and looking at it with hindsight I can see that I was doomed from that point, even though I thought I was absolutely fine. I thought I was in love with Sharon. What we actually had was a dysfunctional relationship and a very damaging co-dependency.

When I graduated from Quinton House after six months I was cocky and full of ego and invited everybody I knew and a few people I didn't to my graduation ceremony so I could bask in their admiration. Naturally my recovery was entirely superficial, as became clear when I moved out of Quinton House and into a flat on my own.

Alone with my thoughts once more, it was only two weeks before the anxieties and self-doubt kicked in again. I only needed a trigger to set me off, and it came when Sharon lapsed from her treatment programme.

This totally devastated me and I reacted like a lunatic. Completely forgetting about my own needs, I ran around trying to fix things for Sharon. I threatened drug dealers with violent consequences if they sold her anything, then used the most twisted logic imaginable to buy some for her myself.

People warned me that I was in danger of lapsing as well, but I didn't listen to a word they said. I had stopped going to my meetings and was angry and resentful that my pipe dream of a healthy relationship with Sharon had been shattered like this. Yet my muddled head convinced me that I was still in love with her.

I had been clean for nine months when I made a momentous decision that to me made all the sense in the world. I would go and buy some drugs for myself, and use with her.

As soon as I made that choice, I felt like a vampire who had been denied any blood for getting on for a year. By the time that I met the dealer and bought the drugs, I am sure that I was salivating. But I could possibly have picked a better drug to make my comeback with than crack cocaine.

Lorraine was not the first – or last – person to tell me that I am no ordinary addict, and unsurprisingly I soon proved the point. Crack and me was a marriage made in hell. As soon as I took a hit off a pipe it seemed to turn me totally psychotic.

Crack is probably the most moreish of all the drugs, and so I went straight back to my old habits of shoplifting and petty thieving to get the cash to pay for it. I looked pretty mental and was behaving the same. Normal people started to avoid me but I didn't even care: all that mattered was getting the money for the next hit.

It also totally reversed my relationship with Sharon, as now she was the one desperately trying to keep *me* off drugs. She knew the last thing my fizzing, troubled cranium needed was a raw stimulant like crack, and she was all too aware of the damage it would do me.

Sharon was vulnerable herself and I was too much for her to cope with. She decided to move back to Ireland to get well again. My first reaction was to think that she was a selfish cow, but, even in my fucked-up state, at a deeper level I understood that what she was doing made sense.

When I waved Sharon goodbye at Bournemouth train station I had never felt so lonely in my life. It was like a stick of dynamite had exploded in my soul. The woman that I loved, and my partner in co-dependency, was leaving me. I don't think I could have felt any emptier or more desperate.

The worst thing was that this awful, heart-wrenching goodbye triggered my memories of being taken to Euston as a kid to wave farewell to my mum as she tried to leave us and go back to Ireland. I might have kidded myself that those memories were buried, but in truth they were never far beneath my surface.

With Sharon gone, I felt abandoned, worthless and deeply unlovable, and began to hate myself with a passion. I didn't find out until a lot later that within a few weeks of getting back to Ireland Sharon was dead from an OD. If I had known that at the time, God knows what I would have done.

In any case, all I wanted to do was to kill the hurt I was feeling – which was why my substance abuse now took a nasty new turn.

As Lorraine had explained to me, my drug taking up until that point in my life had all been about attaining a heightened, stimulated state, but now I wanted the exact opposite. All that I craved was oblivion – which was why I made the mental decision to try heroin.

The first time that I smoked it I absolutely hated it and lost the rest of the day in a wretched, semi-comatose state. That was not going to put me off, though, and I did it again the next day and the one after that. I was willing to persevere if it would take me out of my unbearable life.

By now I hated Bournemouth, myself, everything. I

could not bear to talk to anybody or be around people, so I would hide in my pit all day. I was happiest when I was asleep: when I woke up, a thousand crazy voices chattered in my head. I only left my flat at night, to score smack.

A guy named Steve Spiegel who ran Providence, an excellent treatment centre, took me in, but by now I was too far gone for him to reach me. Instead of focusing on getting well, I recruited another patient as a drug buddy and we ran off to dealers together. The rehab staff were sad to see me fail but they had to protect their other clients, so they discharged us.

With no Sharon and no rehab, there was nothing to keep me in Bournemouth any longer. I decided to head back to the flawed, dirty, dangerous city that I knew and had always called home – London.

This decision didn't bear too much scrutiny. Essentially, I was leaving a sweet, pretty seaside town full of treatment centres and people who were desperate to help me, in order to return to the city where my life had always been chaos, and where virtually everybody I knew was an addict or a career criminal – and normally both. Yet somehow I told myself I had more chance of getting clean there. The power of delusional thinking!

Once back in the Smoke, I stayed with a girl called Tracey that I knew in Ilford. This was a bit of a weird one but I had actually met her through Robbie Williams, the singer. We had all been in a rehab unit together at one point.

Robbie had been a nice guy but fairly quiet, very down to earth. I got on very well with him; he had my sense of humour.

The three of us used to go and smoke together behind the rehab centre around a black drain that had the word 'Angel' on it. I've always believed that's what his song 'Angels' was really about as I heard he wrote it while he was at the rehab with us.

Tracey and I had a bit of a thing and we had kept in touch. She was every bit as addicted as me, but was trying to stop using, so I figured that we could help one another. When I got to Ilford, I found she wasn't getting clean at all – she was bang at it.

We spent every day smoking heroin and crack as if they were going out of fashion. We still pretended to each other that we were going to quit, but the start day was always tomorrow. After a few weeks we got sick of one another and I headed back to my home turf.

A few of my old associates gave me bits of work running drugs around south London, but in truth I was scarcely functioning as a human being. By now I was a full-blown junkie who existed only to find a means, any means, to get his next deadly fix.

Every day was Groundhog Day. There was no social aspect to my drug taking at all: I was using out of sheer necessity. I was totally hooked on smack, and could not bear to waste money on something as stupid and pointless as food if I could spend it on heroin.

It was horrible being under the control of such a disgusting substance. I didn't know why I was taking it every day and I hated being under its influence but I felt powerless to stop. Most addicts take drugs because they enjoy the effects, but I didn't like the smell or taste of heroin or the way it made me feel. This was self-harm, pure and simple.

A new low came when I briefly got involved in dealing and distributing it. Through an acquaintance I had met a gang of smugglers and I was picking up small quantities in east London and distributing them in Bermondsey and Woolwich.

This made me feel even more cheap and dirty, as mentally I never felt that I belonged in this sordid junkie world. I had always viewed heroin as a scumbag substance and I knew the misery that it wreaked on people's lives. I only did it because I was addicted, and being near to the supply chain helped me to feed my own shitty habit.

Thankfully, I didn't sell smack for long. I was so ashamed of what I was doing that I managed to pull myself away from that world. When somebody put me in touch with a dodgy doctor who would sell me morphine pills, it enabled me at least to reduce my dependence on heroin and to function as a criminal again.

I figured that if I could do one last big criminal job, I would be able to buy my way out of my addiction via an expensive rehab. I would never have predicted what kind of job it would turn out to be – and the price that I would have to pay.

BAD TRAFFIC

Just after the turn of the millennium I became involved with a smuggling gang that was working out of a place called Vémars, just north of Paris. Some good friends of mine had been working with them, smuggling cannabis and sometimes people into the UK, and they introduced me to their partners on the continent.

This kind of introduction is essential to get into this business as the smuggling world is incredibly tightly knit. Customs men and security services are always trying to infiltrate smuggling gangs and so the gang bosses are understandably paranoid about working with new people. You have to be introduced by somebody who can vouch for you and give you a good criminal reference.

A friend of mine, Bob Sills, had learned the dangers of infiltration to his cost when he got arrested with 6.5 tons of cannabis off the coast of Littlehampton. Bob had imported the consignment from Spain on a large fishing trawler and it turned out that one of the people on his team was actually a serving police officer. He had posed as a seaman who was open to smuggling, and Bob had made the critical mistake of not doing enough checks on him.

So I had to go for a series of meetings with intermediaries in Paris before I was offered a place on the French operation. I wasn't of sound mind at the time: I was still an opiate addict, just one who was on morphine rather than smack. My job would be to oversee the transportation of the goods to the UK.

We started by doing dummy runs to devise a route into Britain. I would drive empty vessels on recces through different ports, taking very close notice of the customs procedures. My eyes were peeled looking for weaknesses in their operations. In particular, I quickly noticed how short-staffed the ports seemed to be in the early hours of the morning.

We settled on a town called Coquelles near Calais, where lorries would board the Eurostar bound for Ashford in Kent. The next task was to recruit a driver who was willing to drive a 38-ton articulated lorry from Paris to London. This was easy – there was never any shortage of drivers in the London underworld.

The first shipment was cannabis resin disguised in a cargo of French apples. To make this look legitimate, the gang's bosses in the UK had set up a fake fruit company that could supply the necessary paperwork. It worked like a charm. The driver was waved through Coquelles with his fake documents and the dope made it to London, where it was unloaded and distributed.

The European side of the deal was delighted and naturally wanted to go again as soon as possible. Unfortunately for them, I decided to vanish back to London and go off on a celebratory bender. As soon as I had been paid for the job, all of my good intentions of getting clean had been forgotten.

I couldn't help noticing that as soon as I had money again, I also had a ready supply of friends willing to help me party hard and spend it. The cure for loneliness would appear to be money, as it always comes with lots of company attached. In truth, though, inside I was barely holding things together.

When I finally made it back to France, the gang had another job for me. This load was very different: thirty East European would-be immigrants who were unable to get into the UK via legal channels.

My role in the job was to drive the lorry with its human cargo to Coquelles, where another driver would take over and drive it to the UK. I was very uneasy about it. It did not feel right, and I made my misgivings clear in a phone call to one of my co-conspirators. He assured me that it was a one-off as we were waiting for the delivery of a large consignment of cannabis from Holland. However, we had to do this job to keep our continental partners sweet.

I still didn't like it and had no desire to add human

trafficker to my CV but I reluctantly agreed to go ahead. Whatever moral code I may once have possessed had long since been clouded over by my heroin use. I also felt unable to get myself out of the situation. I was in too deep.

The partners we were working with in France were East Europeans and they were not the kind of people that you fuck about with. I had heard a few horror stories in the London underworld of exactly what happened to people who crossed them. The fact of the matter was that when they told you to jump, the only question was, 'How high?'

I wanted out, but it never even crossed my mind to go to the police about the East Europeans. Not only would I have been signing my own death warrant, but I would also have been putting my family at risk of harm, kidnap or torture. I had made my bed and I had to lie in it.

I collected a Volvo lorry with a trailer from a hire company in Calais and followed a black Range Rover to a service station just off the main motorway near Paris. When I pulled off, a hulking East European immediately appeared next to my driver's door and told me to follow him.

I do not scare easily but he was one intimidating fucker. With his piercing blue eyes, he had the demeanour of a man who was not to be questioned. The striking scar that ran the length of his left cheek was clearly a souvenir from a knife fight. Not for the first time, I asked myself: 'What the fuck are you involved in here?'

Another hefty East European took the wheel of the lorry and I was driven in the Range Rover with three other

Slavs to another service station. There, they told me that the plans had changed. I was now to drive the lorry across the Channel myself and would be met on the British side by one of their friends.

I liked this even less than I had the original plan but I also knew that it was pointless and probably fatal to question what they were saying or to refuse. Effectively I was their hostage at this point, and I knew how expendable I was to them.

These savages would have thought nothing of killing me and dumping me in a ditch. Nobody at home knew what I was doing in France except for those people who were directly involved, and nobody knew the real names of the people that we were dealing with.

Everything in this operation was on a need-to-know basis and all you needed to know was your position in the chain and the person that you were dealing with next up the ladder. Basically, if I were to vanish off the face of the earth that day, nobody would be any the wiser. In my long criminal career I have been stabbed and shot at, but I have never felt as frightened as I did sitting in that Range Rover with those monsters.

They could sense I was shitting myself and were toying with me just because they could. 'France is a beautiful country, yes?' one of them said, in his heavy, impenetrable accent. 'It has the lowest detection rate for murders in Europe.' He really needed to work at his small talk.

After what seemed an eternity, I noticed the lorry that I had driven earlier pull into the service station area near to where we were parked. It had a different trailer attached to it now, with the original fixed unit replaced by one with curtained sides. I stepped into the lorry's cab, just relieved to be away from the East Europeans.

The drive up to Coquelles was about three hours long and I was chaperoned the whole way to ensure that I didn't try to abandon the lorry and make a run for it. Every time I looked in my rear-view mirror I could see the Range Rover behind me, with the East Europeans scrutinising my every move.

They had told me to pull into a lay-by just before the port entrance. I did so just before 4 a.m. and was met by another gang of three men in a small Renault. As they approached me, I noticed the Range Rover speed off towards the port entrance.

One of the men in the Renault looked Middle Eastern but spoke very good English and had clearly lived in Britain or studied the language intensively. He handed me a mobile phone and told me that as soon as I arrived in England I should call the one number that was programmed into it. I nodded, he placed a large hand on my shoulder, and I got back into the lorry and drove towards customs with my heart in my mouth.

They say that criminals have a sixth sense for when things are not right. I think this is true. Let me give you an example. A few years earlier, two men I knew had been shot dead while trying to rob a Securicor van. My friend Ollie, who was on the job but survived, said that the moment they had pulled up by the target they had known that something was wrong.

Why? It was seven in the morning and the van they were to rob was in a large wooded area. However, Ollie had immediately realised that although there were trees all around them there was no dawn chorus: no birds singing. The reason was that the Flying Squad had been tipped off about the job and were lying in wait in the woods, which had scared off all the birds. The shootout that followed claimed the lives of two of the robbers.

I had the same bad feeling now. When I drove through the checkpoint and didn't even see one official, I knew that this was an ambush. But by now I was well past the point of no return.

Suddenly a sea of men in high-visibility jackets appeared and ushered my lorry into a warehouse. For a split second I had the idea of jumping down from my cab and making a run for it, but thankfully common sense prevailed, for once. In fact, as I climbed from the vehicle I felt a sense of relief.

'What are you carrying?' one of the customs officials asked me.

'A fucking headache,' I told him.

The customs men opened up the back of the lorry and one by one its thirty-strong human cargo climbed down. They were all East Europeans, ages ranging between twenty and fifty, and all desperate men looking to find work and start a new life. Their dream had just ended right here.

Of course I had never even seen any of them before, and as I glanced over at these desperate, exploited people I felt a tidal wave of shame. It was difficult to raise my eyes from the concrete warehouse floor. What had I been thinking of?

I knew that I should tell the customs men nothing at all. I also knew that I was in more trouble than I had ever been in in my life.

It turned out that I had been arrested in a joint operation by the National Criminal Intelligence Service, Her Majesty's Customs and Excise, and their French counterparts. I was interviewed in France and told that I was being deported to Britain to appear in court as my offence, although committed in France, was against the UK, and Coquelles was a UK-controlled zone.

Before I could be deported, I had to be taken to hospital to be medically assessed. The French police drove me to a medical centre in Calais, regaling me all the way with a string of snide and sarcastic anti-English comments, which riled me no end.

I was desperate to fight them but there were six of them and they were armed and even I could recognise that I would not have stood a chance. Even so, I would have had a good go if they had physically assaulted me. At that time in my life, I didn't always care if the odds were stacked against me.

I was deported under armed guard, and the French customs man told me brusquely that I could not return to France for the rest of my life. This struck me as a bit harsh. I was well used to being barred from the odd pub or nightclub, but an entire country was a first, even for me.

ESCAPE FROM PRISON

Once I had made the madcap decision to escape from custody rather than face my fate for the people-smuggling rap, it had actually proved surprisingly easy. There again, as usual with me it had been a decision made randomly and on the hoof rather than logically or rationally.

Cooped up in Canterbury Prison awaiting my trial, I began to suffer vicious withdrawal from heroin and morphine. I was also having such vivid and intense nightmares every night that I asked to see the prison doctor.

He told me that I was displaying signs of clinical depression (no surprise there) and prescribed some powerful antipsychotic meds. I took them and felt my body slow down but my mind was still racing uncontrollably and I just wanted to lash out at everybody. I was a rabid dog who needed to bite someone.

Outwardly I was putting on the standard prison mask of tough-guy contempt – show no weakness, show no fear – but as soon as my cell door closed and I was alone I was a total mental wreck. I simply could not face being locked up for a very long stretch without my heroin comfort blanket.

My addiction needed feeding and this was impossible inside. It was time for Ray Bishop to fight the system once more.

The security guards at Maidstone Magistrates' Court had not raised an eyebrow when they patted me down and found me carrying my makeshift escape kit of the biro, paper clip and jam sandwich. I had felt guilty about terrorising one of them and taking him hostage in the dock, but really my escape had been surprisingly easy.

Now came the difficult bit. Being on the run.

After I had seen my face splashed all over *London Tonight* on the TV at my dealer's house in Plumstead, I knew that I was a marked man. This impression was confirmed the next day as I skulked down the street trying to look invisible and saw my face staring out of the front of a tabloid newspaper. I hated the photo that they used.

Most criminals who go on the run have some sort of plan – a secret stash of cash or a forged passport to help them get away to a desert island. As my escape had been impulsive and totally spontaneous, I had nothing. The only thing going for me was my wits, and they were pretty fucked up.

I made a few phone calls. A couple of friends lent me a bit of money and I bunkered down at a safe house in Lewisham with a mate's brother. While I was there, most of my family and close friends had their homes raided by the police. I didn't like causing this chaos in people's lives – but I still kept my head down.

My mum begged me to hand myself in and I gave the idea some serious thought. The problem was that I knew I was facing a life-ruining lengthy sentence for the people trafficking even before they added on a few years for the escape. I just couldn't face it – and so I didn't.

Being on the run is a fucking nightmare and I don't recommend it to anybody. For every second of every day I felt intense paranoia and I got virtually no sleep at nights. It was almost impossible for me to go out, as my 'disguise' consisted of no more than growing a bit of stubble and sticking on a pair of glasses. It was worse than Clark Kent in *Superman*.

Past experience had taught me that police raids nearly always happen in the early hours of the morning and so I was up at 5 a.m. each day at my wits' end and ready to flee. Nobody could cope with this level of profound stress and trauma without a little chemical help, and I was self-medicating like mad with whatever came my way.

After a few days I ventured out and, with no other options open to me, went back to my default mode of sneak thieving and shoplifting to support myself. Any money that I got went straight on drugs. It was clearly only a matter of time before I got caught, and it happened sooner rather than later.

Becoming more reckless, I went back to my home turf of Woolwich to pick up some drugs from a mate. As I sat waiting for him in my dodgy specs, a police car slowly drove by me. I clearly should have also invested in a matching fake wig, because less than five minutes later a squadron of armed officers were surrounding me and barking orders.

'Lie on the ground with your hands by your sides!'

For a few seconds that seemed an eternity, I did nothing. I glanced down, and saw the numerous red dots around my chest where their guns were trained on me. Ignoring their commands, I got up, turned around and began to walk away.

Fuck knows where I thought I was going. They charged me and suddenly I was flat on my face on the ground with most of the officers on top of me. I tried to struggle but frankly I had as much chance as a handbrake on a canoe. They slapped me in cuffs and drove me in convoy to Plumstead police station.

When we got there, most of the policemen who booked me in were familiar to me from previous encounters. They were business-like, fair and professional with me. The best cops are often like that. They figure if you are arrested on serious charges, you are fucked already, so why make things even harder for you?

My London criminal mentality also led me to believe that good dedicated cops such as the Woolwich police secretly respect a certain type of villain. Men like me don't burgle your house and I have never harmed a woman or child. We would fiercely protect the elderly and never shit on our own doorsteps. Even when I was refusing to answer a single question the police were asking me, I would talk to them courteously.

Let's put it this way. I am not for one second trying to claim that I was not a criminal scumbag, but I was a long way from the lowest forms of life that these police had to deal with – the contract killers, serial rapists and paedophiles. A lot of these officers had known me since I was a kid. We knew all the same villains, they were part of the same murky world as me, and they had investigated the deaths of many of my associates over the years, and seen some of them turn their lives around. I believe all smart criminals respect the police.

Unsurprisingly I was now deemed to be a high-security, high-risk prisoner and I was taken in cuffs in a heavy-duty secure escort, as they call it, to Medway police station in Kent. A group of officers were waiting for me, and added another line to my ever-growing charge sheet: escape from custody and false imprisonment. The last bit referred to the court guard I had jumped in the dock.

My next port of call was Maidstone Crown Court, where I was forced to wear a bright green and yellow jumpsuit. I had two pairs of handcuffs on and six officers flanked me in the dock. The judge did not even waste time looking up at me as he promptly remanded me in custody pending my trial. I was then whisked away under escort to Elmley jail segregation unit and locked up for twenty-three hours a day.

I had many long dark nights of the soul in that concrete coffin as I reflected on my pathetic life. Throughout these empty hours the voices in my head chirped away at me constantly. My trial was six months away and I was told that I would be allowed no human contact during that time. A

Home Office enquiry into my escape concluded that there was every chance that I would take hostages in another attempt to escape.

I couldn't think for one second why they would imagine such a thing.

The days were long and the nights even longer as my mind wallowed in morbid reflection. A Home Office psychiatrist came to assess my state of mind for the prosecution to use in my upcoming trial. Luckily I understand these people and can communicate with them in their own language.

I have never met a psychiatrist who has not seemed mad to me and yet I always get along with them at some level or other. We tend to understand each other, and the fantastic lady who assessed me for the Home Office, Dr R.M. Bell, certainly went well beyond the remit they had given there.

The report that she wrote read more as if it had been commissioned by a defence barrister than the prosecution. I must have struck a chord in her because she seemed to care for me as a person.

Dr Bell wrote that I was a young man who was desperately seeking avenues of communication. She argued that I could not be held wholly accountable for my actions, as the first instinct of any injured animal is to escape. She added that I had never felt loved or wanted by anybody in my life, and consequently suffered from deep depression.

Dr Bell concluded that at the time of my escape I had been a victim of psychotic depression and was not in total control of my actions. Her assessment had a major impact on me as for the first time in my life I agreed with a psychiatric prognosis of my character. She had hit the nail on the head: I was not well and felt totally lost and alone.

As a result of Dr Bell's sympathetic report, the prosecution dropped the charge of false imprisonment and I pleaded guilty to the lesser charge of escape. This was a significant victory for me. The judge for my trial was one of the people that I had locked in the courtroom when I fled from the dock on my previous visit, so I would not have expected too much leniency there!

Even so, I still left the court knowing that I was going to pay a serious price for my crimes. The judge gave me seven years on the people-smuggling charge and three years for the escape: a total of ten years if there was no remission for good behaviour. I was also fined £60,000.

The £60,000 was worked out at £2,000 per would-be illegal immigrant. Obviously there was no way I could pay it, and the authorities knew that as well – they didn't even bother to chase it. If I ever win the lottery, they might come after me for it. I hope they're not holding their breath.

The authorities also took my passport away from me for ten years. I remember thinking at the time that it wasn't exactly going to impact on my day-to-day life too much.

On my first night back from court I felt a sense of shock and also relief. It's a strange feeling knowing that you have a lot of prison ahead but at least you know how much. In my experience the reason so many lifers go nuts is the fact they never know when or if they will be released.

At least I could start to think a bit more clearly now. Strangely I felt safe in prison, as my life beyond the walls always seemed to descend into chaos. Now I was sentenced it was obvious I was to be transferred to another jail and I would have no say in the destination.

I was on what is known as 'prison hold' as I had an outside hospital appointment to attend first, and my God was this to be a terrible affair. The prison authorities saw this as a chance to display a real show of strength as my case had been all over the local news recently and I was a high-profile convict – the kind they like to make an example of.

Early one morning my cell door opened and I was ordered to put on the same garish yellow and green jumpsuit that I had had to wear to court. Three vehicles full of prison officers accompanied me to Medway Hospital to have my ears looked at as I had a lot of pain in them. Because of my operation as a kid to pin my big ears back I still occasionally get infections in them and I have to go to hospital to get them looked at.

I found myself in a waiting room with twelve prison officers, with me wearing my Coco the Clown suit. I had two by-now-usual pairs of handcuffs on and I was also cuffed to a senior prison officer. These people really were taking no chances and unsurprisingly I wasn't planning on trying to escape.

What happened next was really poignant for me. There was a little boy sitting with his mum in the waiting room and looking over at me. I smiled at him and tried to reassure him with a wink. Our eyes met for what seemed an eternity and I felt something shift inside me.

This boy had a real sadness in his eyes that reflected the sad child that still resided in me. He looked at my handcuffs and grabbed onto his mum with a look of pain in his eyes. In that moment I became a child again.

It hit me hard as here I was, supposedly this terrifying tough criminal and menace to society, and I wanted my mum, too. I would have given anything at that moment to have her love and protection. Dr Bell was right. I had never crossed the threshold from child to adult in any emotional sense.

As I sat there surrounded by my captors, I wanted so desperately to return to the innocence of being a child once again. I had never wanted to enter the adult world that scared me so much, and I felt lost and afraid of the man that I had become.

The shadow I cast was not one that I recognised, and for the first time in a very long time I saw my awful truth. I was in prison with my worst enemy, and that enemy was me.

MAXIMUM SECURITY

The day after my hospital appearance, my cell door was once again unlocked and six officers appeared with a brusque early-morning greeting.

'Get your things packed, Bishop. You're on the move!'

I had no idea where I was going, as you are never told for security reasons. All I knew was that my destination could be any one of the five Category-A jails in the country. These are called the dispersal jails and they are home to the prison system's most dangerous and disturbed inmates.

These glorious establishments house the highest-security prisoners such as terrorists, serial murderers, prolific armed robbers, drug smugglers and organised crime bosses. It was pointless asking which one we were headed to so I just complied and packed what few possessions I had.

All of my worldly items fitted into a large travel box, and my proudest possession by far was a photo of my two beautiful children. I missed them so much every day, and couldn't begin to tell you how many times I had held the photo in my hands to draw strength from them in my darkest hours.

Once I was packed up, I was frogmarched to the reception area to be processed for transportation. Yet again I was double-cuffed, and my fabulous Coco the Clown suit also made another unwelcome appearance. Four prison officers accompanied me into an armoured sweatbox and I felt the rumble of the engine as we pulled out of the gates of Elmley and I watched the world drift past my tiny tinted window.

In my down and damaged state, I was painfully aware that summer was beginning as the trees were a lot greener than when I had first been arrested. I stared longingly at the beauty of the English countryside and, silly as it sounds, I would have given anything to have jumped out and rolled around in the grass for a minute or two.

Impervious to my suffering, my captors sat and chatted jovially as we made our way through the trees and fields. In my mind, the vision out of my window now became that of the life I desperately longed for.

I admired the people going about their business completely oblivious to the troubled young convict being taken fuck knows where. I wanted to change places with them so badly, and my loneliness ached like a scar. I envied the children playing without a care in the world and I swear that I even envied the cattle chewing the cud in the fields.

I envied people's smiles because I had not been on the receiving end of one for a long time. Marooned in misery and self-pity, I envied anybody who wasn't me.

Trying to snap out of it, I focused on the road signs that flashed past the window as I tried to work out where I was heading. I gauged that we were driving west, and after four hours or so we reached the city of Worcester.

At this juncture my heart sank into my boots as I realised what my destination was. Long Lartin Prison was the most feared establishment of the high-security jails. It deserved its reputation as being extremely violent and effectively the last stop before Broadmoor.

Long Lartin is also a first-stage lifer unit, where the courts send murderers to be extensively assessed by psychologists before they are given a more permanent allocation. More than half of its population is lifers and the other half is made up of Category-A prisoners serving long sentences. Fuck! This was a seriously short straw.

I was understandably nervous as I entered the reception area, and the first thing that struck me was how secure the whole prison looked. Wires crisscrossed back and forth across the exercise yard to prevent escapes by helicopter and there were more cameras than on any Hollywood film set.

All of the doors at Long Lartin were operated by a central control tower and the prison officers carried no keys so that inmates were not tempted to overpower them. I also noticed several patrolling officers with angry-looking Alsatians walking about the perimeter wall. I had to wait to be dealt with as another poor bastard was being transferred under armed police guard to another nick.

When it came to my turn, the prison officers in reception were calm and friendly, a fact that betrayed their experience of dealing with dangerous men on a daily basis. This made sense as the majority of assaults on prison staff take place in reception. It usually happens because new prisoners are told that personal items that are important to them are not allowed and the cons kick off when they are told this.

Consequently, the reception staff in dispersal prisons are far more relaxed than is usual. They even tend to offer you a cup of coffee on arrival, which is unheard of in other, lower-security jails.

Naturally, this is not to say that they are soft touches. Prison officers in maximum-security jails are amongst the toughest in the system. Let's face it, they have to be, given the type of volatile prisoners they are dealing with. Many warders are from a military background and have to endure the same stringent security measures as the prisoners do.

I once read that prison officers who work in the dispersal system are statistically the most prone to die from heart disease in retirement. I have no doubt that working in such conditions is stressful to them – but in that case, imagine what it is like for the prisoners who do not get to go home at the end of every day!

After being searched I was allocated to A Wing and

walked up a series of corridors to my new home. On the landing I was struck by the length of the sentences displayed on the cell cards. Most were saying life, and all of the fixed-termers were in the range of ten to as much as thirty years.

I felt the steely glare of the other inmates as I walked on the wing but I did not feel intimidated. By now I had become hardened to prison life, and I understood the peacock dance amongst prisoners when they had a new arrival. Fortunately for me some south London faces I knew were on the wing so I felt OK.

Ray Betson, who had attempted to steal the De Beers diamond from the Millennium Dome in an audacious robbery, was there, as was my friend Ollie, who had survived the shoot-out at the botched Securicor van heist. Another good friend, Gary S from Deptford, was also on A Wing, having recently received eighteen years for robbery.

There were some very dangerous men on my wing, including terrorists and men convicted of contract killings and other truly heinous crimes. In the face of all of this, you would expect the atmosphere to be tense and hostile. However, what was amazing about Long Lartin was how relaxed it actually felt, as everyone seemed to get on just fine. Inmates were allowed to cook for themselves and they all seemed to look out for each other. It had the feeling of the very last thing I had expected – a community.

I was to understand the reason for this far better as my stay went on. Unlike other, lesser-category prisons, all of the men here were doing very long sentences, and as a result they had to live alongside each other for sometimes decades. This meant that they really got to know their fellow cons and could adjust to whatever mindset they were in as they knew them well.

I would go so far as to say that, consequently, dispersal prisoners are the best lay psychologists I have ever met. You are always in a heightened state of risk assessment in such a dangerous environment, and you become very in tune with people's moods.

It was not uncommon for men to spot when someone was in a bad place and they would adjust their behaviour around that person accordingly. Don't forget, I am talking here about real genuine psychopaths who could quite easily kill you and not bat an eyelid. Some of the men on my wing had killed more than once and showed no signs of remorse yet were able to pick up on these nuances of mood in their fellow prisoners.

What has always struck me about this type of person is how normal they tend to look and behave. You really would not spot them in your midst, as they are the proverbial man next door. During my stay I talked to many of them. Some had been told that they would die in jail.

Surprisingly, then, there was far less malevolence and violence in Long Lartin than I had expected. However, when it did break out it was pretty nasty.

Over the years there had been murders committed in the place, and prison staff had been assaulted so badly that they had been forced to retire. Even in my time there I witnessed several stabbings and more than a few serious fights, which were mostly linked to the illicit drug trade.

Once, down the gym, I saw a man with his stomach cut clean open and his intestines hanging out. He was a member of a gang in Birmingham who was serving life for murder. One of his victim's family members was from a rival gang and also in Long Lartin, albeit on a different wing. He planned his attack well and cut him up good and proper as they passed each other during a gym session. It was not a pleasant sight at 8 a.m. as most normal people are settling down to tea and toast.

For my part, I had no serious trouble in Long Lartin as I was trying to sort my life out and kept away from the illicit drug scene, which was where most of the trouble seemed to kick off. I had no enemies that I knew of in the place and I tried my best not to make any in such a dangerous environment. I was smart enough not to invite trouble to my door.

But make no mistake – had it come to my door, then I would have done what I needed to. I made a commitment to myself years ago that I would be no one's victim. Dangerous men all have one thing in common, and that is our eyes. We all have a steely glare when we get wound up, and this is the point where it's sensible to back off.

On a few occasions in Long Lartin I gave people that look – the one that says 'Don't fuck with me!' – when I was getting pissed off. Luckily they backed off, because I always had a tool close by, and I would not have hesitated to use it. Like so many of my fellow inmates, I was still an untreated damaged child and capable of extreme violence.

The jail was rife with weapons of all kinds and inmates had them hidden all over the shop. Part of the prison regime was a metal workshop where inmates could learn the art of welding. Unsurprisingly, many prisoners seized the opportunity to make homemade knives and other weapons.

These would then be smuggled out of the workshop and back onto the wings. Prisoners are ingenious when it comes to hiding things and there was many a weapon concealed on my wing. The toilet cistern was a favourite spot, as was the exercise yard. Inmates also hid knives in flowerbeds to be retrieved when needed.

The scariest factor was that there was no shortage of dangerous men in Long Lartin capable of using those weapons. Once while I was there the officers searched the yard with metal detectors and recovered over 100 homemade weapons. It's a terrifying thought given that half the jail was in for murder.

Only a fool would underestimate a dispersal prisoner, as purely by the fact of being there we were all considered dangerous at some point. I witnessed many so-called hard men from lesser jails turn up with a muggy street attitude. They would soon be reduced to their right size, because in dispersal prisons it doesn't matter who you think you are – someone will still do you if they feel like it.

Psychopathic people do not care if you are a gangster or a hard case, as they do not feel fear as normal people do. So these foolish men with their belief that reputation or muscles would keep them safe often got taught a harsh lesson.

On one occasion a flash chap turned up from a B-cat jail, all pumped up with ego and muscle. He was loud and obnoxious to the older respected faces on the wing, perceiving them to be no threat. What a fool. A face put a contract on him: in other words he put a price on his head for anyone willing to do him.

There was no shortage of takers and a big Geordie called Whizz took the £200 bounty. It may not seem a lot of money, but to a smackhead psycho in a dispersal prison it is a life-changing sum. Two hundred pounds will buy plenty of heroin to be getting on with.

On the way out to exercise one morning I saw Whizz pull a table leg from his jacket and smash the target clean over his head. The guy was out cold with blood spurting out from a gaping head wound. We were all swiftly locked up while he was rushed to hospital.

We never saw him or his muscles again.

I tried to follow the example of the more sensible prisoners. There was a kind of con that I really respected: the sort of heavy-duty criminal who held his water, was dignified in the way that he conducted himself and never complained about his lot.

I mean people like Rookie Lee, Kevin Lane, Michael and Martin Valentine and Billy Tobin – not forgetting Wilf Pine and Vic Dark, who weren't in Long Lartin. They have always been real faces, proper chaps, who I have looked up to in life, and in prison I tried to follow their lead. I was tight lipped and lived by the staunch prisoner's moral codes. I was always polite to my fellow con and made time for people whenever I could.

Consequently, I was accepted by, and became friendly with, some very well-respected people. I was on good terms with members of the Russian and Turkish Mafias, for example. These guys were taking organised crime to a whole new level and they intrigued me deeply.

One of the Russians was doing twenty-five years for the importation of over £100 million worth of cocaine. The Turks were all in for heroin smuggling and money laundering and their sentences ranged from twenty to as much as thirty-five years. As with all those chaps, you never heard them moan once.

I also became very friendly with a guy called Pat who was in the Real IRA. He was a particularly high-risk prisoner who was serving thirty years for a series of car bombings on the British mainland. In his most notorious attack, his cell had targeted the main BBC news centre in White City. They had placed a car bomb in a taxi in Wood Lane outside the studios and it had detonated, causing widespread damage although nobody was killed.

I stuck up for Pat one day against another con who saw him as being a target because he was of very slight build. I felt the need to defend him for two reasons. Firstly, I hate bullies; secondly, although I am not political, I am still half Irish. My loyalty is divided between England and Ireland and that is fine by me.

Pat never forgot this and assured me that he would always watch out for me if I ever needed it. For his part, the con who had threatened him soon found out what a mistake it was to cross a member of the Real IRA. Shortly afterwards, one of his close family members was approached in the street and issued with a death threat by a man with a strong Belfast accent. The con never bothered Pat again.

I became close to many a big-name English gangster and armed robber during my time in Long Lartin. I met many men that I had read about in the newspapers and found them to be very different to what I would have expected.

John Palmer was on my wing for a long time and I found him to be a very pleasant man. John was infamous as being the alleged launderer of the Brink's-Mat gold bullion robbery. He had been found innocent of this charge but nevertheless acquired the nickname Goldfinger. John was doing eight years for what was reported to be the biggest timeshare fraud on record out in Spain. He was rumoured to have a personal fortune of over £300 million.

Another man that I got very friendly with was a guy called Steady. Steady was from Manchester and was serving a life sentence for armed robbery and murder. He had spent a lot of time in special units owing to his propensity for sudden and extreme violence. For some reason, he and I hit it off from day one and were like two peas in a pod.

Steady's case was a tragic one for all concerned. Along with a friend, he was a highly active armed robber in Manchester in the 1990s. He was robbing a Securicor van outside a bank when his gun accidentally went off. The bullet hit a security guard in the head, killing him instantly.

Obviously, the fact that Steady was holding a loaded .357 Magnum meant that he was a disaster waiting to happen. The media had a field day, reporting that it had been a cold-blooded execution as the security guard had tried to grab the gun in a misguided act of heroism. They painted Steady as a clinical, heartless killer.

This could not be further from the truth. I talked to Steady in detail about the killing, and he was consumed by remorse. I saw him shedding bitter tears over his victim when he talked me through what had happened. He had only been twenty-five years old at the time and the parallels to my own life were astonishing. That was why we were drawn to each other.

When I met Steady he had already served over eleven years. His life sentence had come with a recommendation that he serve a minimum of thirty years before being considered for parole, and he was still categorised as a high-risk Category-A prisoner. He and I hung out a lot with a guy called Eddie Smith.

Eddie was serving ten years for shooting a man with a shotgun. He and I got on extremely well owing to the fact he was from the travelling community. Ever since I used to spend my nights with the local travellers around Abbey Wood and Thamesmead as a teenager, I have always had strong affiliations with them and I understand and respect their ways.

Their whole lifestyle is based on loyalty and respect and looking after their own. That is why you do not see many skint travellers, as on the whole they distribute their wealth fairly. Eddie loved me and we used to really have some great laughs together.

Another of my closest Long Lartin friends was the notorious Lenny Kempley. Len was a high-risk Cat A serving eighteen years for a series of armed robberies. During one of them, things had gone drastically wrong. He and three accomplices had been relieving some industrial premises of a serious sum of money, and when the police had turned up to arrest them a car chase ensued.

During this chase Lenny and his gang had opened fire on the police in their bid to escape. No one got hit but this raised the stakes for them massively. It is one thing to do an armed robbery, but once you start to discharge your weapons it is a whole new ball game and you know it is not going to end well. Either you are going to be shot and killed by the firearms unit sent to nick you or you are going to get arrested and spend decades behind bars. Don't believe for one second that the police always shout warnings and shoot to disable. If they need to shoot they will, and do, and they are usually trained to kill, as many British criminals could attest if only they were still alive.

Two of the more high-profile prisoners that I encountered were Jeremy Bamber and Barry George. You certainly could not have met two more different characters.

Bamber was doing life for shooting dead five members of his own family at White House Farm in Essex in 1985. He had initially claimed his sister had done it before turning her gun on herself, and had continued to claim his innocence, launching a series of appeals.

Bamber was not popular in prison and got assaulted quite a few times. He had a very grandiose, narcissistic manner and looked down on all the other cons. He also had a nasty, psychopathic temper – I saw him turn one day just because another inmate had used his oven ring in the prison kitchen. He struck me as a very dangerous man, and to my mind he was guilty as sin.

Barry George (whom I met in Belmarsh, not Long Lartin) was totally different. He had been convicted of shooting dead the TV presenter Jill Dando on her doorstep in Fulham in 1999. Not one person in prison, con or screw, believed he was guilty. He spent his time in jail harmlessly wandering the landings.

As it happened, I had already been told a very plausible tale for what had happened to Jill Dando. During my time in Spain, I had befriended a Bosnian Serb guy who was working as part of the Albanian Mafia out there.

This guy told me that Jill Dando had presented a TV charity appeal for Albanian refugees that had really pissed off a Serbian warlord leader called Arkan. This guy had ordered a high-profile hit on Dando. The forensic evidence certainly supported the theory of a professional hitman. Barry George was in fact acquitted of the murder in 2008, though the case remains unsolved. I guess it is likely to stay that way.

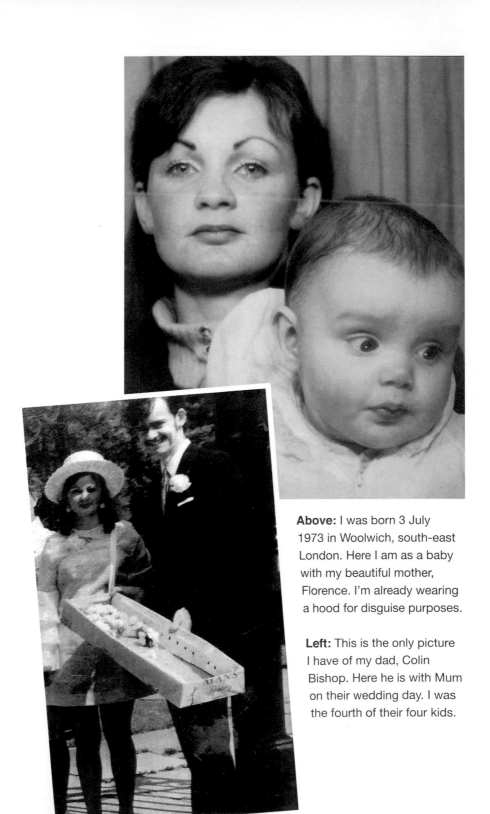

Above: I was born 3 July 1973 in Woolwich, south-east London. Here I am as a baby with my beautiful mother, Florence. I'm already wearing a hood for disguise purposes.

Left: This is the only picture I have of my dad, Colin Bishop. Here he is with Mum on their wedding day. I was the fourth of their four kids.

Top left: HMP Grendon, 2003, with Mum, my stepdad and beloved Biscuit.

Top right: Me with the world's most beautiful woman, my Sammy.

Left: Me and my good friend, author and fellow south Londoner, Noel 'Razor' Smith. We first met at HMP High Down in the 90s and ended up at HMP Grendon together.

Below: On a family day at HMP Grendon in 2003, with Mum, my beautiful daughter Leeanne and son Ashley.

Box it SMART RAY.
WeLL CHUFFeD Jou. MADe GooD..

Left: My dear friend Charlie Bronson drew this for me. He's often misunderstood and sensationalised by the media. I've seen another side to him.

Right: Big Jem Newman (left), my closest friend and a man who has been there for me all the way, and the legend that is Wilf Pine (right), one of Ronnie and Reggie Kray's most trusted confidants and former Mafia associate.

Below: The formidable Lee Murray (left) and Paul Allen (right). Good friends of mine, currently serving 25 years for robbing a Securitas depot of £53 million, Britain's largest-ever cash robbery.

Above: In action against Frankie Brooks in 2008, a true warrior from Pompey. It was my night that night. The referee, Andy Walker, is one of the best in the business, so was the MC that night, Steve Holdsworth.

Top: Ringside at Upton Park to support Kevin Mitchell against Michael Katsidis in 2010. With (left to right) Chalky, Huey Delaney and Jason Rowland, who fought Ricky Hatton in an epic battle.

Middle: Friends and associates, including Big Jem, Jimmy Fox, Brian Watts, Lloyd Coates, Richie Kilpin and Peter Ling, coming to watch me box.

Left: With boxer Frankie Gavin. Unbeaten to date and English boxing's first ever world amateur champion.

Above: With southern area champ, Roger Dorway, on my left, European kickboxing champ, Marcel Kelman, on his left and Joe Marino, USAF boxing champ, far right.

Left: With the legendary Big Jem (left) and Danny Arkins (right), a great boxer and former coach at The Golden Ring in Southampton.

Below: Roger Dorway, Big Jem and me at R&R Boxing Academy Bournemouth, a club that Roger, Stuart Maroney and I started. It's still going to this day.

Above: Me training with former British, European and World champion, Cornelius Carr.

Right: Up 300ft on top of a church I had scaffolded. My Everest.

Below: Terry Akusu, a great man and great counsellor, with Danni Constantinou, probably the best psychotherapist to ever work with me. I shall always be in her debt. A truly amazing woman whom I will always love dearly for the effort she put into getting me well.

Above: WCBC British Super-middleweight Champion. The culmination of dedication and hard work in the ring and outside the ring. A proud moment.

A
TASTE
OF
HONEY

Although I fucked about a lot at the beginning of my time at Long Lartin, I knew that I had to make this sentence work for me. My plan was to address my offending behaviour and educate myself.

I sometimes draw on wise quotes that I have heard in the past for guidance. The infamous Charlie Richardson had said in an interview during his 25-year sentence that if you take your mind beyond the wall, then your body will surely follow. This made sense to me, and prompted a decision in me to use my grey matter for once.

As a result of my engaging with my sentence planning – the process of going through my long-term goals with the prison staff, and agreeing to the courses and drug rehab programmes I needed to achieve them – the Long Lartin psychology team put together a package to support me. They were in favour of my security risk being downgraded to Category B so that I could go to another prison and attend drug courses.

After I had been in Long Lartin for a year, I was offered a place in a new therapeutic community in Dovegate jail at Uttoxeter in Staffordshire to address my drug addiction and repeat-offending behaviour.

I was in two minds about this. One reason was that Dovegate was a fairly new facility and I thought it was bound to have teething problems. My other objection was geographical. Dovegate was even further north than Long Lartin. My mum only managed to get the kids here to see me three or four times a year. If I went to Staffordshire it would be even harder for her.

Nevertheless, it was an opportunity, and I wasn't getting too many of those nowadays. After a few days of deliberation, I accepted the place and was transferred.

On arrival at Dovegate, I reaffirmed my commitment that I was going to settle down, remain drug-free and pursue an education. I applied for funding to the Open University and could not have been more excited when I was accepted.

I was to study for a BA Hons degree in psychology and I was now more determined than ever to make my sentence serve me well. Completely free of drugs, I was thinking a lot clearer and for the first time in my life I felt genuinely optimistic about my future.

I also started to engage in therapy but it was all so strange and unfamiliar to me at this point. My natural resistance to change was still very strong and I treated it all as a bit of a joke. I was too anti-authority in my attitude as I still had a lot of fight in me. I simply did not see the point of the therapy, especially as I figured that I knew for a fact that I was OK now.

Remember, crazy people do not walk into the doctor's surgery declaring that they are mad. The same as in Bournemouth, I could not accept that my mind was still distorted as I believed that not taking drugs was all it would take to straighten me out. Sadly, I had underestimated my addictive insanity, and it was soon to rear its ugly head again.

When I had been in Dovegate for a short while I started to feel strange and disconnected. My mood was shifting from positive to negative and I was increasingly resentful about being there.

There was a group of lads from Toxteth in Liverpool in the unit who were using drugs, and up until this point I had avoided them. However, something changed within me and I started to become friendly with the gang.

My attitude had changed and although I was still studying hard, I had lost the urge to remain drug-free. As I tried to look at my emotions in therapy, the old urges and cravings started to build up in me. In no time I was using whatever I could get my hands on. With my thinking once again warped by drugs, I told the wing psychologist to fuck off.

My flashpoint came during a lunchtime when I took it upon myself to attack a fellow inmate that I had taken an extreme dislike to. In our therapy group, this man had owned up to exposing himself to schoolgirls and this had totally done my head in. In my twisted criminal code this was unforgivable, and I could not bear to be around people like him.

My attack was pretty brutal. I smashed a jar of honey over his head, and when a friend came to help I hit him in the face with a table tennis bat. The friend fell unconscious to the floor. It all happened so quickly, and while it was going on it felt like I was in someone else's body.

It is strange but whenever I have been extremely violent in my life I have felt very different from what you would expect. I do not feel anger and rage – I act very calmly, and this was no exception. It really did feel like I was not in active control of myself during the assault, as if I was acting on autopilot.

Once again my crazed mind had sabotaged my chances of getting the help I so obviously needed. I returned to my cell to await the inevitable swarm of prison officers descending upon me. Shutting my door in an attempt to hide from the world, I lay on my bed.

The darkness that lay within my mind began to chat with me. It was laughing as the gravity of my actions began to sink in. I knew that I was in deep water as this would inevitably lead to further charges. The only way that I knew to counter the feelings of remorse and guilt was to put on my prison mask yet again. When my door eventually swung open I just lay on my bed like I did not have a care in the world. Shit. Who was I fooling?

I got whisked away to the segregation unit to await my fate. A senior officer told me that one of the inmates I had beaten up was pressing charges against me and that the North Derbyshire Police would be coming to interview me in the morning. I was in deep trouble, as another violent conviction would see me sentenced to a two-strike life sentence.

The way this worked was that anybody who was put away for a violent offence – as I had been, for my courtroom escape – could be hit with a discretionary life sentence if they committed another violent crime. It was a horrible thing to have hanging over you – and it looked as if I had just triggered it.

This had been one of the many negative and backward-thinking moves introduced by Tory Home Secretary Michael Howard. He also introduced mandatory drug testing in jails, which simply meant that cons changed from smoking dope, which stays in your system for twenty-eight days, to heroin, which will be gone inside two. At a stroke he created a whole generation of junkies. Something of the night indeed!

As I lay on my bed in the block that night after I had decked the flasher, I thought, 'Well, this is it, Ray – game over!' I tried to contemplate my fate and my life, and a huge sea of quicksand surrounded me. I didn't particularly care about myself but I did care about my children and my poor mum. Why did I put them through this? I wallowed in self-pity.

Fortunately for me, the policeman who turned up to interview me shared my strong dislike of men who expose themselves to schoolchildren. Before our interview, he briefed me with a statement that he strongly advised me to adopt as my own.

The cop recommended that I claim I had been forced to defend myself against this big man who had tried to drag me into his cell to do God knows what to me. I would say that I had been walking down to the hotplate with a honey jar in my hand at the time, and had lashed out with it in self-defence.

The officer suggested that there would be hardly any evidence to go on as no other witnesses had come forward, and nor were they likely to. The offer to help seemed too good to turn down and I grabbed it with both hands.

After I had spent three weeks in the Dovegate segregation unit, my door was unlocked and I was taken before the jail's governor. He informed me that due to lack of evidence the police were not pursuing the allegation of GBH made by the Feltham Flasher.

I felt a massive sense of relief (not to mention an even deeper sense of gratitude to my Derbyshire Police saviour). This meant that I still had a release date to work towards, and I was now more determined than ever to knuckle down and get on with my sentence.

However, I was not to have it all my own way, as during our meeting the governor also informed me that the Home Office had reviewed my security status and was reallocating me back to a maximum-security establishment. I was to be held at Dovegate in segregation until transport arrived at some point in the near future.

I thanked the governor and returned to my isolated home in the block. My mind had seemed to calm down a lot since my latest outburst. I think I had become resigned to my fate and in some warped way I had given up hope. Nevertheless, somewhere inside I felt I was worth more and the fighter in me began to resurface, but in a more positive way.

There is a prison superstition that whenever you leave a jail you must always eat your breakfast before you go. The legend runs that if you don't you will find yourself returning to eat it at a later date. I really should have munched down mine when I had left Long Lartin a few months earlier.

LEAVING LONG LARTIN

As my sweatbox pulled in again through the daunting gates of Long Lartin I felt the windows in my soul close with a corresponding clang. Here I was once again in the oppressive high-security institution that betrays the beauty of the Worcestershire countryside. I stepped from the mobile cage and into the reception area with my shoulders stooped and an upside-down smile on my face. Instinctively, I knew that I was going backwards.

There were six reception staff waiting to greet me and escort me to the security control and care unit. This is the term used for segregation in the high-security estates as they are filled with the *crème da la crème* of the British penal system. The governor of the unit met me there and informed me that I was to be kept in isolation until members of the psychology team had done a fresh assessment on me.

I was allowed my coursework and toiletries and again stuck in a cell for twenty-three hours a day. I became determined to study and get good grades in my Open University psychology degree, and I threw myself into my course work with a new and invigorated passion.

I was finding this course fascinating and rewarding. I wrote a lot about child development, evolutionary psychology and behaviourism. Particularly, I found myself drawn to the neo-Freudian idea of communication below the level of consciousness.

At the same time, I took an English A level. I enjoyed Chaucer and Shakespeare but didn't care at all for Elizabeth Barrett Browning and her sonnets. She may be a classic writer, but I thought she was a right fucking morbid old bird!

My only freedom from my cell was a daily shower and half an hour's exercise in a small concrete yard. From my window, the vista was truly stunning. To my left: a CCTV camera and an infrared lamp. To my right: the unforgettable sight of the perimeter wall.

Yet the one thing that no one can ever take away from a man is his imagination. An addict's mind has no difficulty in escaping from whatever harsh reality he is in as fantasy is our default setting. If we do not have a substance at hand then we often float off into an imaginary world of our own creation.

I would alleviate the boredom by drifting off into the majesty of my life-long passion, the universe. I daydreamed

about floating around the stars and planets and I contemplated the many cosmological theories in existence. I was well
versed in such matters, as I have always been obsessed with
the universe and its many mysteries.

Occasionally the monotony would be broken by the
visual treat of a seagull landing on top of the prison wall. I
could see nothing green or natural whatsoever and so I would
spend hours dreaming of the beautiful sea and coastline in
Bournemouth. In my mind I would walk along the beach and
see birds and blue skies all around me.

I dreamed of laying on the sand and the sun shining on
my face. I could hear the waves gently rolling onto the beach
and the sound of children's laughter as they played freely. How
I longed for freedom from this concrete hell.

As I gazed around my primitive, limited accommodation, it dawned on me that I was in the bowels of the prison
system. All around me were lost souls and I pondered how my
mind had led me to a place where my heart did not belong.

Many times I prayed long and hard to a God I did not
believe in. Inwardly I began to search for the softer side that
I knew I possessed. I had not always been a bad man, I told
myself repeatedly.

In this total isolation an internal dialogue had begun,
and my soul – for want of a better word – was starting to communicate with me. I did not recognise the voice as it was soft
and gentle, unlike the harsh grunt I was used to hearing. It's
a strange thing, but since then, whenever my back has been
really against the wall, the soft voice inside has seemed to

guide me out of whatever hole I have fallen into. Yet all I knew at this time was that I hated going through life as me, and I dearly wished that I was someone else and somewhere else.

Next door to my left was a serial killer, Bob Maudsley, who had killed four people including one inmate in Broadmoor and two in Wakefield jail. To my right was a Scouser who was on a dirty protest and smothering his cell in his own shit. I remember thinking that I would not be knocking on the neighbours' doors to borrow a cup of sugar.

An animal rights protestor had starved himself to death in this same segregation unit. He was serving fourteen years for a series of attacks on animal testing laboratories. I am not going to name him out of respect for his family, but I will say that his courage knew no bounds and I learned a lot from his spirit. The morning of his death filled me with great sadness as he died for a cause that I also hold dear. I am not an extremist but I believe all animals are God's creatures and should not be subjected to any cruelty.

Two months into my stint on the segregation unit, an officer called Cheryl from my previous wing came to see me. Cheryl was a beautiful Welsh woman who had earned the immense respect of pretty much every inmate in the prison. She was strong but fair and she understood the men that she was entrusted to keep in order and look after.

It seemed that some of the good old London chaps such as Kevin Lane and Rookie Lee had persuaded Cheryl to try to help me. She asked me if I would behave myself if she were able to get me back on the wing, as there was no doubt that she would be sticking her neck out on my behalf and it would look bad for her if I took the piss and lamped somebody else.

I looked Cheryl in the eye and made her a promise to behave immaculately and partake in all of my psychological assessments. I meant it as well, as I had done a hell of a lot of soul searching during my time in isolation.

The result of my internal conversation was that I had decided that I was really going to try my best to change. I was going nowhere in life and this awful truth was with me every time my head hit the pillow. Conscience was fast becoming my greatest pursuer and there was no escaping it – no matter how hard I tried.

The psychological assessments that followed were the most in-depth I had ever experienced. Over a three-day period, I spoke in depth to a psychologist about my hopes and fears. I also relived much of my life in the hope that she would find a way to fix my broken mind. I spoke about my addiction to the drugs that were plaguing my life and the fact that every time I took them I turned psychotic. I tried to explain how I felt emotionally but did not find it easy.

The psychologist could see that I did not have the verbal tools to fully describe what was going on inside me. She asked me question upon question and took copious notes. At the end she promised that she was going to assist me in any way she could. I trusted her smile as she closed her folder and left the room we had been in for what felt like weeks.

Now that I had done my assessments, the governor agreed that I could leave segregation and return to communal life in Long Lartin. It was made clear to me in no uncertain terms that any more trouble would mean isolation again. I did not want that so I decided that I was going to do all I could do to better myself. I read lots of self-help books from the library, and studying became my drug of choice.

I was now over two years into my degree and my mind was being opened up academically. I would spend hours studying and obsessively writing essays and I achieved fantastic marks. This boosted my self-esteem and I became addicted to the buzz of a good grade.

Studying psychology was also opening my eyes to possible interventions to solve my own problems. I was starting to feel that maybe I would benefit from some form of therapy and decided that I was going to stop fighting against the idea that it might actually help me.

I knew that I had wasted so much of my potential by being a criminal and drug addict. However, I also knew that I was not stupid and I had hopes and dreams of living a normal life. All around me in Long Lartin were men that I had once looked up to and aspired to be like, yet now I could see that I was worth so much more.

Suddenly I could see their unhappiness and I felt the human tragedy of many a sad case around me. I was certainly not looking down my nose at anyone in prison, but in my soul I now knew that I was different. My soul was crying out to me that I needed out of this lifestyle and I had finally begun to listen to it.

The psychology team suggested to me that intense psychotherapy would help me with my problems. Now that my psychology studies had opened my mind to the idea of psychotherapeutic intervention, I saw the potential for change and I agreed to sign up for the two years of therapy.

Examining the options available, I decided to put myself forward to go to HMP Grendon in Buckinghamshire for two years. Grendon is a unique jail. A Category-B prison, it works like a therapeutic community, with its inmates able to exercise a large degree of control over their day-to-day lives. They can even vote each other out of the place.

Prisoners who go to Grendon have to commit to therapy groups and to constantly analysing their previous behaviour and crimes in an attempt to improve and turn their lives around. For me, applying to go there was a massive decision as it represented the fact that I was turning away from criminality and all its warped codes.

Unfortunately, there is a certain stigma attached to Grendon as some old-school, misinformed convicts just view it as being full of nutcases. Sadly, this prevents many prisoners who could benefit from it from applying, as they do not want to be regarded as crazy.

However, I was finally developing the capacity to be honest with myself as the life I had been living to date could only be described as insane. The desperation in me to better myself now far outweighed any concerns about what other people thought of me. I just knew that being me was painful and I was sick and tired of harming people and not feeling like a part of society.

My decision to go into therapy was probably the greatest step from insanity to sanity that I have ever made. Despite this, I found it really hard to tell my friends in Long Lartin of my decision as I had grown so close to many of my fellow prisoners in my time in there.

As I have said, long-term prisoners are a different breed of con and you forge close bonds with the men that you are incarcerated with. Leaving them behind to progress in my sentence was never going to be easy, especially when some of those I was leaving had very little hope of any progression for years to come. However, my decision was made and it felt right for me so I set about telling all those I was close to.

Considering the type of inmate that I was surrounded by, the support for what I was doing was overwhelming. My date of transfer was set for early June 2003, and as it approached I made it my mission to say my farewells to all the men I was leaving behind in this high-security human graveyard. I was leaving behind a world of living nightmares. It had been an education, to say the least.

I knew in my heart that this time I would not be returning, and I was finally killing any idea within me that this sort of place was where I belonged. I spent my last night in Long Lartin in quiet reflection as I contemplated the road ahead.

I did not expect it to be easy at Grendon as I knew I was in for some deep soul-searching. I sat and ate a last meal with my lifer mates and relived some of the laughs we had shared together. I have a tendency to make people smile at their most difficult times and some of them told me that was what they would miss about me most.

It has been my lot in life that I often find I make people

laugh when I am trying to accomplish serious things and I am not trying to be funny. I can just be a bit clumsy in my approach to things, which can result in me leaving a trail of comical errors in my wake.

I was reminded of the time I had agreed to paint our wing with Steady. I thought it would be quicker if I threw the paint at the walls and then rolled it. Apparently I was not supposed to paint the floors as well and I had been given loss of earnings as punishment.

There had also been the time that I had found an injured pheasant in the exercise yard and decided that I was going to keep it as a pet. Strangely the bird recovered its ability to fly and the prison authorities had to get a specialist in to catch it as it nested in the Long Lartin roof.

Then there was the time that I had decided to redecorate my cell by emptying the entire contents out of my window. It had been raining that night and I naively hoped that I would get a load of brand-new furniture. The authorities had not take kindly to this initiative and I spent a couple of weeks in the isolation block for that one.

On yet another occasion I somehow convinced the screws that I had once played guitar in a band and I wanted to start teaching my fellow inmates to play this lovely instrument. Impressed, they had allowed me to have a guitar posted in. Naturally I could not play a chord, and I swapped it for a bit of puff.

It was funny at the time and alleviated the stress and the boredom of being banged up, but looking back I was acting out the role of the rebel during this period in my life. I was still a confused young man who was very much the actor playing up in front of his mates and gaining self-esteem by making them laugh. For a while, it got me through the day – but it could only ever be a short-term solution.

It was funny reminiscing with my mates and it softened the blow slightly that I was leaving them behind. I retired to my cell that night for the last time and I lay on my bed in quiet reflection.

I certainly had some good memories and some bad ones of my times in maximum security at Long Lartin. I had been surrounded by men whose cases I had often read about in the newspapers or seen on the news. When you got to know them, none of them were anything like their media portrayals. Looking deeper, I could also detect the damage they had suffered that had often propelled them to commit their crimes.

Contrary to popular belief, most murderers have very deep remorse and regrets. A lot of the men I met had underlying issues themselves that were unresolved. I am not making excuses for their actions but many that I spoke to had mitigating factors as to why they had snapped at some point.

A very high proportion of lifers had been a part of the care system as children. Many of them had awful experiences there. I cannot imagine what it must have been like to have been placed into care as a child and then been abused, often sexually, by those who were supposed to be caring for you.

Only those with the cleanest of hands deserve the right to point fingers. All too often the newspapers claim prisoners have no remorse and are all living in the equivalent of five-star luxury hotels. It is obviously their agenda for you to think this, as it could not be further from the truth.

What the media do not cover so much is stuff like how high the suicide rate is, especially among long-term prisoners. Guilt and remorse cripple many convicts. I have seen men have breakdowns of all sorts in jail. Some are transferred to mental institutions and lost to society for years.

I have also witnessed some of the very worst kinds of self-harmers in jail. I met one inmate who told me that he had once cut his stomach open so badly that part of it had to be removed. Inevitably, he turned out to be another product of the great British care system.

I have also met countless other men who should not be in prison because they are innocent of their crimes. When you are around people for twenty-four hours a day for a long time you get their measure. Of course, there are those who falsely claim innocence, but you can usually tell they are faking it.

But what about the genuine ones who get locked up? I spent a lot of time with one prisoner called Bob Maynard. Bob had been convicted of two murders in the 1970s and had always protested his innocence. I believed him as I got to know him on a profound level and I could see he was not capable of such an act.

After I had moved on from Long Lartin, I watched a *Rough Justice* television programme about his case. It was being reopened as a result of new forensic testing that had not been available at the time. His conviction was subsequently quashed on appeal and he was released from jail a totally innocent man. It had taken twenty-five years of wrongful imprisonment to clear his name.

Long Lartin taught me to never judge a man by his history and his conviction but to judge him by his level of remorse and willingness to change. I met so many prisoners there that, given the chance, would probably go on to be useful members of the societies they had harmed. Sadly for some of them this chance would never come, and I considered how fortunate I was to be leaving.

I decided that I would carry a piece of all the good men that I had met as I left this jail for a new life. There were, of course, plenty of other men that I was also glad to leave behind. Some terrorists and murderers in there feel absolutely no remorse at all, and they are the ones that should stay there.

I awoke on the morning of my transfer to Grendon feeling anxious but also strangely excited about what lay ahead. I renewed my commitment internally and said a prayer for strength before grabbing all of my belongings and being escorted to the reception area for transport.

The prison officers on duty wished me well, and I think they meant it. Cheryl came down to reception and instructed me to buckle down and behave myself, as she did not want to see me in this place again. I enjoyed being scolded by this beautiful woman, and the naughty child who is never far beneath my surface replied with a cheeky grin.

GRENDON CALLING

As the van pulled out of Long Lartin I felt an enormous sense of relief. I might have got used to life inside its walls but that doesn't mean it hadn't been incredibly stressful.

In high-security prisons you feel more than ever as if you have to behave in that showy tough-guy way. You have to keep your prison face on at all times, and it takes a mental toll on you. As I sped through the streets in the sweatbox, I felt as if I could finally breathe out and relax.

Looking through the van windows, I loved the sight of trees and flowers again rather than concrete and barbed wire. It felt like nature was making a special effort for me as I gazed at the blue sky, clouds and cows as we passed through the Worcestershire countryside. The journey took two hours and in a strange way I relished every minute.

The good vibes continued when we arrived at HMP Grendon. If I thought my welcome at Long Lartin had been surprisingly civilised, this was something else. The officers waiting for me in reception weren't just warm and friendly – they called me 'Ray'.

This was a first for me as before then I don't think I'd ever been anything in prison other than 'Oi! Bishop!' I realised there and then, as I sipped the coffee they had just handed me, that this place was going to be all about therapy and not punishment.

The officers told me that I would spend an initial 28-day period on F Wing for assessments and drug testing. Everything at Grendon happened on a voluntary basis, but obviously I agreed – after all, that was what I was here for, to stay clean and turn my life around. In any case, if I hadn't agreed I'd have been packed straight off back to Long Lartin.

The F Wing tests were to determine whether the inmates were actually ready to enter therapy. Let me tell you, it is no easy ride. Suddenly opening up after years of repression and fear can push some people over the edge. For me, I thought I would be OK. I had been pushed over so many edges over the years that the only way left for me to go was in a positive direction.

Dr David Jones, a senior psychotherapist, welcomed me to F Wing and explained what was expected of me and what was on offer if I engaged well with my treatment. I assured him that, I meant business and was willing to do whatever I

GRENDON CALLING

could to change my ways. His response was to smile and say that, with the right attitude, a change in my behaviour could happen in spite of me.

I set my few belongings down in a small cell that was just like all the many other cells I have occupied, and ventured out to meet my new social circle. Having heard many scare stories about Grendon being full of total nutters, I had been expecting to see some real weirdos. It came as a surprise when they all looked fairly normal.

I felt very reassured to see my good friend Razor Smith there. Razor is a staunch prisoner who has had tragedy in his life. While he was serving his life sentence for armed robbery his teenage son, Joe, had died, and this disaster tore Razor to pieces and led him to decide to challenge his criminality by entering Grendon and therapy.

Two more friends of mine from Long Lartin were also there, which made me feel even happier about my decision. Darren was an ex-soldier who was serving a life sentence for killing a sex offender. He was a tall, highly intelligent man who had served his country with pride, but sadly was having far more trouble winning the war against his own personal demons.

The other guy that I knew, Richard, was also serving life after accidentally killing another man in a fight. He was from Peckham, another south Londoner like me, and well known for being hotheaded and prone to violent attacks on authority figures (it was hard to see why we had bonded, but we had!).

I met plenty more people that I warmed to in there, of whom the most unlikely was Kevin. This was a weird one for

183

me as Kevin was a dedicated neo-Nazi skinhead and my own political beliefs could not be more different. Yet I could see something in this confused man that intrigued me and I spent hours talking to him. He fascinated me on many levels.

You won't be surprised to learn that I have always loved a rebel, and Kevin was certainly one of them, but he also had a contradictory air of kindness. I felt immediate parallels with my own life, as here was an angry, confused man desperate to be liked and accepted by people.

Unfortunately for him, his edgy skinhead appearance frightened people away. Kevin was later to tell me about the terrible abuse he had suffered as a child that had fuelled his warped racist beliefs, and after that he made a lot more sense to me.

There was a wing at Grendon full of sex offenders, but the other prisoners didn't integrate with them. This pleased me as I hated these monsters with a passion and had never had any understanding of what drove them. Nevertheless, I had to grudgingly give them credit for coming here to try to address their sick behaviour.

Even so, I knew it would be a test for me to occasionally bear being around those people. In the past, if I had had a chance to get near any of them, I would just have caved their heads in. That had been drummed into me in past prisons. It was the world I came from.

But I engaged well on F Wing and my head felt clearer than it had in months, mainly because I was off drugs and determined to remain that way. Obviously it meant I had the time and clarity to reflect on the issues that were being raised in my therapy sessions, which were often challenging. Having no TV in my cell also meant that I could get on with my degree course without being distracted by *EastEnders* and *Coronation Street*.

After the 28-day assessment period I was allocated to the C Wing therapy unit. This was a bit of a result as it meant that I would be billeted with Razor, Kevin and Darren. It also had a reputation as one of the best wings in the nick.

On arrival on C, I met two other lifers who I already knew from knocking around the prison system – Freddie and John.

They both had reputations as being good cons and they filled me in on the wing and gave me the usual rundown on who was there. There were forty inmates who were split into five groups. Thirty of them were lifers and the rest were fixed-termers.

In charge of the wing were a psychotherapist called Andy and a psychologist called Jenny. Another psychotherapist, Liz, facilitated a lot of my therapy groups. They were a formidable team and quickly earned my very deep respect.

I would not have been able to imagine saying this in any other nick, but the prison officers on the wing were also a great bunch who went out of their way to support the prisoners in therapy. One particular officer, Paul Johnson, must have helped more men not to reoffend than any man alive.

A great example came when one of the Grendon prison staff took a CD off me. Old habits die hard, and I jumped over the counter to smack him one. Rather than putting me into a headlock, Paul Johnson grabbed me and yelled at me, 'Where are you now?'

This threw me and I felt totally confused and vulnerable, but I guess it was brilliant therapeutic work on my anger issues. Paul was wise enough to know that I was reliving aspects of my bullied childhood. In any other establishment this behaviour would have resulted in me being dragged off back to the segregation unit, probably getting a kicking along the way.

Instead, Paul put his arm around my shoulder and walked me back to my wing without as much as a telling off. He encouraged me to go back to reception and apologise to the officer I had threatened, and when I did I felt a release of so much hurt and pain. In that moment I experienced from Paul what I had missed, and craved, my entire life – the feeling of being fathered.

My group facilitator was the psychologist, Jenny, and I took an instant liking to her, as she was warm and bubbly with a good sense of humour. I was also very pleased to see that she had a lovely arse. In fact, I think that seemed most important to me!

I had known the group therapy sessions would not be easy, and they were not. It was incredibly hard to open up about all the demons in my memory and my soul. The dad who had walked past me in the street and ignored me; the bullying and loneliness I suffered as a kid; the years of confusion, drug abuse and self-loathing. Slowly, haltingly, it all came out.

When you look hard in the mirror, you don't always like what you see. Sometimes I would go back to my cell after a group session and feel sick to my stomach, as if I was actually going to throw up.

I even went to the prison doctor, saying I must have irritable bowel syndrome – but he couldn't find anything. Eventually I mentioned it to my psychotherapist, and he said, 'It's where your emotional world is, Ray.' He said this emotional upheaval and change could actually cause my physical pain. I had that for most of my first year in Grendon.

I didn't mind the rest of the group members except for one feller. He had killed a woman and her two children in a fire and it killed me to have to listen to his stuff in the group sessions, but I knew I had to find a way. Whenever he spoke I had to switch off, as it was the only way I could deal with the urge to throw him in the bin.

A lot of therapy sessions involved listening to graphic accounts of murders from the men who had carried them out. It was often a horrific experience. This was not the movies! It was hard for me to hear these stories without feeling sadness for their victims, and for how their families and friends must have suffered.

At the same time, I gained a deeper understanding of what had driven these men to kill. Many of them – possibly the majority – had been seriously abused as children and were filled with an anger that I could relate to.

For the first time, I realised that in the right – or wrong – set of circumstances I could easily have killed somebody before now, and this thought terrified me.

It brought home to me just how much I had previously

lived in the grip of an uncontrollable rage. From that point, I doubled my efforts in therapy to challenge any violent urges that welled up in me and to explore the underlying factors.

In that first year in therapy I really examined my whole life in fine detail. I also had the added luxury of spending hours with my tutor, Dr Page of the Open University, who had a knowledge of addiction that was second to none. Amazingly, this uneducated south London kid who had left school clueless and angry was *en route* to a first-class honours degree.

Then, at Grendon, I was to meet the best friend that a man could ever have. His name was Biscuit.

Biscuit was my pet budgie and I raised him from a chick as his mum had thrown him out of the nest. I fed him with a cotton-bud pipette and watched him get big and strong. Biscuit loved me immensely for it and never once tried to fly away.

This may sound crazy, but when Biscuit was an adult he would even try to feed me back. He would fly over to me, sit on my shoulder and put seeds in my ear. If I were away from C Wing for too long, he would fly around looking for me. It was like being married, although I was a far better partner to Biscuit than I had ever been to a woman!

Ask any inmate about a prison budgie and they will tell you the same thing. The birds live alongside us 24/7 and act like humans. When not caged, if we whistled for them they would follow us anywhere and sit on our shoulders.

When the therapy sessions were tough, I would spend countless hours at night playing with Biscuit as I unwound and recovered. In the budgie world, he was a right chap, with a vocabulary second to none. He could say his name and he knew more swear words than Gordon Ramsay.

This may sound stupid to normal people but Biscuit was a real help to me in the change process. Before then I had been incredibly selfish and put my needs before anybody else – full stop. Yet here was this vulnerable, delicate creature totally dependent on me to survive.

It's weird that it took a budgie to teach me to consider the wellbeing of something other than me, but that was how it worked out. I'm glad to say that Biscuit was well looked after – in fact, I spoiled him rotten.

Yet he couldn't restore my delicate mental equilibrium on his own. At this stage, for all of the care and therapy I was getting, I was basically still completely nuts and I felt that I needed something to replace the stimulation and intensity that taking drugs had given me.

As I had done in Bournemouth, I turned to the gym. I decided that I was going to get super-fit and managed to secure a job as an orderly in the prison gym. This time I decided to go a stage further, revisit my youth and take up boxing again. In no time the idea obsessed me.

Luckily, there was no shortage of training partners who also fancied a bit of boxing in Grendon. Freddie and I and a few other lads on C Wing decided that a large spare room on a nearby landing would be the perfect place to set up a boxing gym.

We could only imagine the number of objections that our therapists would have raised to this scheme so we decided not to tell them. This was our little secret. We made pads out of old mattresses and a punchbag from a large kit bag. Not having gloves, we wrapped prison T-shirts around our hands.

In no time a hard core of us were whiling away many an afternoon and evening in our makeshift gym, punching lumps out of each other. I loved it, particularly as the idea had always nagged at me that I had wasted the boxing talent that I had had in my youth.

Inevitably, though, the wing therapists became suspicious as several of us simultaneously began to materialise for group sessions with black eyes, cuts and bruises. Our secret got discovered and the gym was forced to close down.

Even so, it had been good while it had lasted, and I continued to train in my cell and in the prison gym. I still had a lot of fight left in me and I needed some way to channel it, and for me boxing was perfect.

I was doing so well on the drug-free front that I decided I was going to do something positive in recognition of being two years clean. Another inmate, Darren R, and I decided to start a discussion and activity group called Breaking the Chain.

The thinking behind this group was to encourage fellow inmates who had experienced addictions to get actively involved in their own recoveries. We had no access to any of the twelve-step fellowships so we decided to do something similar. It just seemed that the therapeutic value of one addict supporting another in prison could be immense.

Darren and I set about arranging a seminar that we were going to present to the therapy staff and inmates as well as the prison governor, Dr Peter Bennett. Dr Bennett liked the idea and gave us a budget of £500. We decided the format should be speeches by two inmates about their personal experiences of the consequences of addiction, and a talk on relapse prevention. The £500 paid for a buffet.

On the day of the seminar the conference suite was packed with all sorts of dignitaries, doctors, therapists and even representatives from the Home Office. What's more, over half of the prisoners at Grendon attended, although we obviously knew that some of them had only come for the buffet!

When the seminar got going, an inmate called Lee shared his experience of growing up in a tough part of Glasgow and being a criminal from a very young age. His addiction had taken hold in his teens and he was now serving a life sentence for killing his own dad in a drug-fuelled rage. He told his tale through tears of sadness and remorse, and it was hugely moving.

Next came a lifer called Graham who had been in prison for more than twenty years. Graham shared with us that he had been abused terribly as a child and had taken to drinking to block out the pain of this trauma. After he became an alcoholic, he had blacked out and shot and killed a young couple in a lovers' lane. Graham felt incredibly guilty and sorry and accepted that he had little chance of release.

The seminar listened to these terrible stories of lives ruined by drink and drugs in rapt silence. I don't think you could have heard them anywhere but HMP Grendon. Our event was turning out to be enormously powerful.

Next came a presentation on relapse prevention, and a

lifer called Gordon had compiled a slide show to accompany this. This all took place in the middle of a display of poems and short stories written by the inmates. As we socialised with our guests at the buffet at the end, we thought it had gone pretty well.

We weren't the only ones. What followed was amazing for us. The experts who had attended praised us to the skies for having done something unique within the prison system. Dr Bennett gave us all a little bonus and the Prison Reform Trust even awarded me a laptop to recognise my attempts at rehabilitation.

This was all very new for me and I found it really humbling. It just felt good to be doing something useful for a change and I knew instinctively that this was to be my path out of criminality. It was such a buzz to get recognised, along with my fellow prisoners.

Now that we were on a roll, we started up an inmate Drug Strategy Group. The idea was that we would hold regular meetings and look for ways to aid our personal recoveries alongside the treatment we were already getting. We implemented a buddy scheme for men who wanted to talk in confidence about their drug and alcohol problems, and we advised and encouraged them to talk about it in their groups.

This might seem like overkill given that all these men had come to Grendon to try to change anyway. However, many of the inmates would avoid any talk of substance abuse in therapy if possible. Most were serving life sentences and they feared that if they talked about their desire for drink or drugs it would set back their sentence plans. But they responded to the buddy scheme and it was a success.

By now I had never been happier in my life. My relationship with my family was good and my friends both inside and outside were all supporting what I was trying to do in recovery. At thirty-three years old, I felt like I was finally starting to live.

Although I was more than four years into my sentence, I was still classified as a Category-B prisoner, which meant that I was held in pretty high-security conditions. This bothered me, and I asked the wing therapist about the possibility of being downgraded. He told me that he agreed, and wrote a report to the Home Office on my behalf.

Consequently, my security status was downgraded to Category C. This meant that, should I wish, I could apply to go to a semi-open prison on completion of my therapy process. This made sense, since as a long-term prisoner my aim was to get to an open prison to be a halfway house and help me to acclimatise to the outside world before release.

However, something inside me had clearly changed. After two years in therapy, I was given the dual option of going to a Cat-C prison now or else staying in therapy for another year and going to an open prison at the end.

After thinking long and hard about it, I decided to stay in therapy at Grendon. It was a bit of a no-brainer. I could see just how the place had benefited me. I was now three years drug-free, in my last year of my psychology degree and had picked up other qualifications, including a drug-counselling diploma. Staying there made sense: it was also possibly the first properly adult decision I had ever made.

Because of this, I was even allowed to further my own rehabilitation by leaving Grendon (accompanied by prison officers) to give talks at schools on the perils of crime and drug abuse. I gave a whole load of these lectures and found them incredibly rewarding.

It was a bit more of a challenge when I got asked to take part in a debate on corporal punishment at Grendon Prison with Professor David Wilson from Manchester University, a leading criminologist. This expert has forgotten more about crime than even I will ever know and has assisted the police and FBI in forensic profiling, as well as making a TV series about serial killers. Despite being against corporal punishment in reality, I was asked to argue for the position of bringing it back, which I did as best I could with my limited debating skills. So it was pretty amazing when I beat Professor Wilson on an audience show of hands – even if I did suspect I was getting a sympathy vote from the prisoners. It is still a bit of an in-joke between us now.

I also got to take part in a debate with the then Labour government minister for prisons, Paul Goggins. I argued for a greater need for resettlement prisons for inmates coming to the end of long sentences as compared to the crazy Tory policy, much loved by Michael Howard, which could essentially be summed up as 'lock them up and throw away the key'.

I also pointed out to Goggins the damage some of his own party's policies had created. One of the main ones was to do away with all home leave for long-term prisoners. The result of this was that they were being released with no re-adjustment period or acclimatisation, which made them far more likely to reoffend.

I tried to explain that, in my own experience, my recidivism had been based on my struggles to readjust to life outside. Goggins listened to what I had to say intently, and the next day there was a picture of him with some of the inmates in the *Guardian*, taken by a journalist who had accompanied him there.

It finally felt like my life was going the right way, and at the beginning of 2005, after two and a half years in treatment, I was downgraded to a Category-D status. This meant that I could finally apply to an open prison for the last year of my sentence. It meant a lot to me – as did the reports that I received from Grendon.

My final therapy reports were incredibly moving and it was hard for me to accept and make sense of the positive things that eminent psychotherapists had written about me, praising my commitment and contribution to treatment in HMP Grendon. Once again, it was a totally new experience.

All my life to that point I had only read negative things about myself. The most extreme point had been TV news shows and tabloid newspapers warning the public that I was a maniac who should not be approached. However, even before that I had been a nuisance to the authorities, as detailed in countless police and court reports.

I knew those reports had been founded in truth: after all,

I had been a violent, drug-addicted waster at the time. Now I felt vindicated as I held these new, complimentary reports in my hands.

My final port of call for this long stretch was to be HMP Latchmere House in Richmond, Surrey, just south-west of London. This was as good as it could get for me as it was London's only resettlement prison for long-term inmates. The plan was that I would slowly reacclimatise from prison life as inevitably, after five years, I was fairly institutionalised.

The regime at Latchmere would also allow me to work outside the prison, which meant I could hopefully save up a bit of money for when I got out. After all, this made it far less likely that I would revert to my default criminal ways. On some days, I even dared to think that the future looked bright – but as the transfer date of August 2005 neared, I grew ever more nervous.

I know how weird this sounds but I felt sad to be leaving this particular prison behind. Grendon had changed my life. I had gone in through its gates a frightened, disillusioned kid, and I was leaving as a relatively confident man. In a funny way, my therapy had been like a second chance at childhood.

In my three years there I had grown fond of residents and staff alike. My views on life had changed dramatically and I now felt a sense of hope and ambition. No longer hooked on drugs and criminality, I felt confident that I had worked as hard as I could on all these issues.

Had it worked? Only time would tell.

When it came time to say goodbye to the staff and

therapists, I found it incredibly moving. We had grown up together. It was like leaving family behind. I had received such love and support there that it was a real wrench – and frightening – to let go.

One particular thing showed me the massive changes that had occurred in my psyche. Wherever I had been banged up, I had always hated prison officers with a passion, viewing them as bastards and the enemy. At Grendon, I was saying goodbye to some of the people who had supported me through my darkest days in treatment.

When I came to say farewell to officer Paul Johnson, I put my arms around him and hugged him. He had done so much for me and so many men like me. As I said, during my time in Grendon he had been the thing that I had never had in my life – a father figure.

Paul had taught many men like me who hated prison officers to see beyond the uniform. His efforts and those of others had even shown me that warders were not all bad, and some even cared about the men they were banging up – and those were not words I thought I would ever use. As we went our separate ways, he patted me on the back and told me to fly the nest and build a life for myself.

They were lovely words. It sounded a fantastic idea. Now all I had to do was work out how the fuck I was going to do it.

OPEN CONDITIONS

I was used to being shuttled around between the nation's prisons in a sweatbox under heavy armed escort. The way that I left HMP Grendon was rather different.

The Home Office let me know that they would trust me to make my own way to Richmond and HMP Latchmere. This went against everything I had ever known about the prison system but it seemed significant to me. I arranged that a good friend of mine, the boxer Huey Delaney, would come to pick me up and drive me the two-hour journey to Surrey.

It was no surprise that I felt anxious as I left the reception area at Grendon. I had not set foot in the outside world for nearly five years. Despite my uneasy relationship with religion, as I left I looked back, thought of all the men I was leaving behind and said a silent prayer for them, as well as asking God to give me the strength to continue on my journey.

I had made sure my best friend was going to be OK. Biscuit was safely tucked up in his cage and was going off to live with my mate Danny in Bournemouth. There was no way I was leaving him in jail so today was also release day for him. Biscuit and I spent many long nights together in Grendon and he had seen me at my worst. His reward was to be budgie freedom and a new life by the seaside.

I had thought a lot about what it would feel like to be in the outside world again but even so I found that I had seriously underestimated the shock value. On the most basic level, it amazed me just how busy and purposeful everybody seemed. It was also a revelation to see beautiful women everywhere again – and a very welcome one.

Everything felt new, fresh, and strange. It was weird to bend down and feel grass in my hands again, and to cope with basic things such as holding money and using it. When Huey and I stopped for some food on the way, I struggled to eat with a metal knife and fork. I was so used to eating with plastic ones that they kept falling out of my hands.

It was all disorientating and overwhelming, and secretly I felt what a lot of long-term convicts feel when they are finally released – that I could not wait to get back into the safety of prison again. In my case, Latchmere.

Of course, I knew this was a major challenge. Latchmere was an open prison but it was still a mainstream jail, full of cons with no interest in therapy and rehabilitation. There would be the usual skulduggery here, and tests would come thick and fast for me. I took a very deep breath before I entered the induction wing.

Inevitably, what happened was what happened every time I went to a new nick – several inmates who had been banged up with me elsewhere before recognised me and came over to greet me. Instinctively, I felt like going into the default mode that had got me through so many stretches before and putting on my prison mask.

But I was a changed man and I managed to fight that urge. Instead, I spoke to them politely and courteously and even stayed away from our usual conversation topic of crime. In the past, it had been all I had ever talked about. Now, it seemed boring to me.

It's amazing how most cons in jail do nothing more than swap tales of criminal exploits. I'd go so far as to say that some of them simply couldn't talk about anything else. As I had been, there are mentally addicted to criminality, and while they are that way, they have fat chance of reforming.

Put simply – you are as you say you are, and if all you ever talk about is crime, how the hell are you going to change? It's hard to say which prisoners are the most depressing – the ones who are sitting out whole-life tariffs, or the ones who are recidivists and just keep appearing again and again.

I have always had a deep terror of becoming an old lag who never knew any life but prison. I have met hundreds of these people, and I can assure you they are nothing whatso-ever like the jovial habitual criminal Norman Stanley Fletcher from *Porridge*. They have a deep sadness in their eyes that no masking smile can hide.

I started my spell in open prison in a very positive frame of mind. No longer driven by guilt and shame, I felt free from the burden of my mind for the first time in years. I was also still enjoying being drug-free, and I was allowed to protect this status by attending Alcoholics Anonymous meetings.

This abstention was not to last. Despite my new confident veneer and sense of wellbeing, my same old self-esteem and fear issues were still bubbling within me. I quickly noticed a lot of men in Latchmere who were pumped and looked physically super-toned from their trips to the gym. It might be stupid – well, it is – but I felt inferior to them.

These men looked a lot bigger and more developed than anyone I had seen in prison gyms over the last five years. When I got friendly with a few of them, I soon found out why. Latchmere was awash with anabolic steroids, and as soon as the dormant addict part of my brain learned this fact, I was craving them. I wanted in.

Naturally my mind had got a very good cover story. I told myself that steroids would not be like taking drugs at all. Of course this was complete horseshit, but like all addicts I can be very seductive, and soon persuaded myself that it made a lot of sense to start injecting myself with testosterone.

This made me feel incredibly aggressive all the time and in previous years it would have turned me into a ticking time bomb primed to go off at the slightest trigger, but after all of my therapy at Grendon I was at least able to channel it better.

Instead, as I had in Bournemouth, I became totally fixated on the gym, working out for two hours every single day.

It obviously had an effect. Pumping that much iron while also gobbling steroids, my whole body shape changed and in no time at all I looked like a condom filled with walnuts. It also made me feel strong and invincible, but once again all I was really doing was building muscle to mask my fears. The child who was desperate to be loved donned a grotesque hard shell to keep everyone away.

I didn't know then but I do now that I was doing what is called cross-addiction, when a previous substance of choice is replaced by a new one. Not that this was anything new to my OCD character – I had always taken loads of different drugs at the same time.

Latchmere House required all inmates to work for the first six weeks in the grounds of the prison. After that, you were allowed to apply for a paid job in the community and gain experience of an honest day's work. Once a week, you were also allowed to take a twelve-hour town visit, as it was called, with your loved ones.

The arrangement was that you would leave the prison at eight in the morning and not have to return until eight at night. You had to carry a licence from the jail explaining that you were allowed to be out, and you weren't allowed to go more than 25 miles from the prison.

As my first town visit neared I was incredibly apprehensive. Little things like walking down a street that ordinary people just took for granted had now become daunting for me. A few times I even caught myself dreading what should really have been an exciting and rewarding adventure.

That Saturday morning my mum arrived to pick me up and take me out, together with Leeanne and Ashley. All of the nerves I had been suffering fell away as I stepped through the prison gate on a glorious sunny morning to be greeted by the three people that I loved the most in the world.

I ran to my children and scooped them up in my arms. As I looked into their beautiful faces I felt such profound, contradictory emotions. The depth of my love for them was amazing, and yet I also felt deep shame that I had let them down so badly.

Leeanne and Ashley had been small innocent children when I was arrested for the people-smuggling job and now they were both teenagers who had grown up knowing their dad was locked away. At that instant, as I gazed at them, I understood more than ever the truth of that old maxim that crime doesn't pay.

I wondered if they were looking at me and also going through deep and confusing emotions. They must have thought that I looked older and battle scarred from my time inside. But could they sense the change in me – that I had begun to come to terms with my flawed and vicious nature?

I was a different man from the one they had waved good-bye to when I was locked up. I had been away a long time, and sadly it had coincided with the crucial, formative years of their lives. I could do nothing about that. But if I couldn't change the past, at least I could try and do a better job in the future.

We did such ordinary, routine family things that Saturday, but it felt like a day in paradise. The four of us went into the nearby town centre of Kingston and, after mooching around the shops for a while, we ended up in a cheap-and-cheerful Chinese buffet place for lunch.

It was hardly Nigella Lawson fodder but even so I found it hard to eat as my body was not used to what was rich, high-quality food by my normal low standards. The *Sun* and *Daily Mail* would have you believe that our prisons regularly serve up Michelin-star quality food to their pampered inmates. Let me tell you, in the more than twenty different jails I have been in, I have never seen a menu that would even grace a burger van.

After lunch we went for a walk in Richmond Park. I could not have been more proud as we walked around the gorgeous setting with Leeanne's delicate hand in mine and Ashley making me laugh with his witty, dry comments. Even my long-suffering mum seemed to be happier as I took my first stroll away from the watchful gaze of prison warders for five years.

I had suffered an absentee father of my own, so even though I loved my kids and our circumstances were very different, I was still aware that I had caused stress and pain in their lives. I had chosen to be a career criminal; their own crime had been to love me, for which they had served a sentence of separation. None of it had been their fault. I was so grateful that they had not given up on me, and we could still bond.

Back at Latchmere House that night I was exhausted. The day had totally drained me emotionally and I was asleep before my head hit the pillow. The next morning, however,

I had something to look forward to: my new job in the prison aviary.

Latchmere House had an amazing collection of birds of prey and I fed and cleaned them every day. I absolutely loved it and grew very fond of the birds. We had hawks and buzzards, but my favourites were two eagle owls. Both were big enough to kill rabbits, and the female weighed 15 kilos. Imagine having her sitting on your arm, with her talons that could tear your flesh open!

Eventually Latchmere House informed me that, as part of my rehabilitation and acclimatisation process, I could start looking for employment in the community. If I found work, I would be allowed to leave the prison at 5 a.m. and return at 7 p.m.

The only trade I had was scaffolding, and a mate who owned his own company in Wimbledon, fairly near by, offered me some work. So I got into a routine where I would leave the jail at dawn every morning, graft all day and in the evening clean out the aviary and go to the gym with my mates.

The scaffold world is a tough one and it is not for the faint hearted. However, it has always suited me as I have no fear of heights – or, indeed, anything – and at the time I was in Latchmere House I was so pumped up on steroids that I was incredibly strong. If fact, I suppose I viewed the labouring as yet another training workout.

I would go so far as to say that I am fairly infamous in the scaffolding world. Mention my name to a London scaffolder and the chances are that he will have a story or two about me. I was so reckless that people would say I belonged in a suicide squad.

One time I worked without a harness on a TV mast that was 800 feet up in the air. I've got a photo of me standing on top of a church steeple totally unsupported. Another time I hung over the edge of a 200-foot building on a beam in an act of lunatic bravado.

Looking back, I guess I still wasn't mentally well when I was doing all that shit, but at least it helped the days to go by quicker. The weird thing was, there were so many nutters and people with a screw loose working as scaffolders that my behaviour didn't always stand out all that much.

I had to laugh at some of the places I found myself working in my new job. Talk about ironic! I had a history of armed robbery and was on day release from prison, and yet there I was erecting scaffolding around the Royal Mint, the Bank of England and the Israeli Embassy, with its armed guards watching over us.

I even worked unsupervised some nights in the Tate Gallery, surrounded by millions of pounds' worth of paintings. Had I been so inclined, I could have put one under my arm and literally walked off with it.

Luckily, I was more concerned with taking the piss. My worried boss had told me to be extra careful not to damage any of the artworks, and I couldn't resist phoning and saying that I had had an accident, and had Rembrandt painted any spares?

The highlight of my week was still my town visit, which I would take on Saturday. If I wasn't seeing my mum, Leeanne and Ashley, I would go down to Bournemouth and spend the day with my mates or hang out with a girl that I had met down there.

Whenever I was in Bournemouth, I would always call round to my friend Danny's house to play with Biscuit. He was in good form and enjoying his retirement by the sea, playing with his toys and sitting on top of his cage and talking to the plastic bird I had given him in Grendon.

I loved the fact that Danny could leave every window in his house open and Biscuit never once tried to fly away. I felt proud that I had trained him so well in jail, where I would always leave his cage door open to give him the choice of being in or out. I had figured, why should he try to escape when I gave him everything he needed, and loads of love as well? Biscuit clearly felt the same.

Back in Latchmere House, my parole date was fast approaching and I sat down with the prison staff to write a series of reports. I had to detail where I would live and what I would do if I were released, and the Home Office would then decide whether to release me or make me do another year in custody.

I explained that I intended to go to live with Danny down in Bournemouth and then had an anxious wait while I waited for their decision. Yet it wasn't as simple as me dying to get out of there and dreading being cooped up for longer. In my head, it was as lot more complicated than that.

Long-term prisoners call it gate fever and a lot of us get it as we near the end of our sentences. Basically you get anxious and get the fear as the prospect of leaving what you are used to looms in front of you. Life in prison can be limited, but it is also regimented and orderly, with a comforting routine.

Still, news came through that the Home Office had okayed my release and I would be out in six weeks on parole. As the day neared, I grew increasingly nervous and apprehensive. In a stupid way, I had dreamed of freedom for so long that now it was becoming a reality I felt robbed of my escape fantasy.

I was excited but also confused: after all, I didn't really know what I would do with myself when I got out there again. I phoned Danny, who reassured me that everything was going to be OK and I shouldn't worry about a thing. At least I had a staunch friend waiting for me.

As we chatted, Danny told me that he was suffering a lot of pain from emphysema and so was taking strong painkillers. He said that he intended to attend a rehab in South Africa and was going to go before I came out of the nick and went to live with him.

I spoke to Danny again a few days later and he promised to call me the next day to let me know exactly when he would be flying out there. It was a bit of a strange conversation and I went to sleep that night with a feeling of unease that I could not have begun to explain to anybody.

The next morning another mate, Peter Gravitt, called me with devastating news. Two friends had gone round to see Danny and found him dead in bed. At first I didn't believe it, didn't want even to entertain the idea: how could this special, loyal friend be gone, just like that?

When it sank in, it hit me hard. With no idea how to handle the pain, I wanted to lash out at somebody – at anybody. I couldn't find any words, couldn't shed a tear, couldn't eat anything. Instead, I just sat on my prison bed in a state of complete shock.

Danny had never let me down and I would have trusted him with my life and with my deepest, darkest secrets. As I ached at this horrible tragedy, the only slight comfort I could find was that Biscuit would have been with him when he drew his last breath. I hated the thought of him dying alone.

I was allowed out of jail for Danny's funeral, which was a mammoth affair as he was a very well-respected chap from Islington. The church was so packed that a lot of the congregation had to stand outside. Our mutual friend Mark Dunford, whose wife is Linda Robson off of *Birds of a Feather*, paid tribute to him and there was not a dry eye in the church.

After the service, I hugged Danny's son, Lawrence. I had no words to ease his pain – there were none – but at least I could tell him that Danny had loved him with all his heart, always talked about him, and was proud of the man he had become.

That night, back in Latchmere House, I lay across my bed and wondered just what the future held for me now. Danny had been like a brother to me and I had put all my eggs in one basket when planning to rebuild my life at his place in Bournemouth. Now he was gone and that was all bent out of shape.

Should I go back to London instead? Instinctively that didn't feel the thing to do. I decided that I would stick with the plan of moving back to Bournemouth and I would take a place in a probation-run hostel there. At least I still had a few mates in the town who would support me and help me stay clean.

Even so, I was now so terrified of my impending release and freedom that I could not even think about it clearly for more than a few seconds. Mentally I was really struggling. I even seriously thought of doing something stupid to sabotage my release, so I could stay where I felt safe and looked after.

For the last couple of weeks I was on autopilot as I did my scaffolding job during the days and took refuge with my birds of prey in the evenings. I spent long hours watching these noble creatures and fearing for my immediate future and what it might hold.

Much as I wanted to, I couldn't stop the hands of time, and my last night on the wing was truly painful. It was hard for me to say goodbye to my mates and work colleagues and it would have been even harder to say goodbye to the hawks and eagle owls. In fact, I just couldn't do it: it would have cut me up too much.

I think also part of me knew, in the back of my mind, that I wasn't leaving prison in quite the shape I could be. I was not taking any drugs such as coke or weed, but even so I was still gobbling steroids as I pumped iron frantically down the gym. Occasionally I'd suspect that this maybe wasn't a great idea, but I would quickly disregard this thought and go back into denial.

Despite my own abstention, I had also fallen into the role of being a middleman for various dealers that I was locked up with. In short, I had made great progress while in therapy, but a leopard does not change his spots that easily. I was slowly falling back into my bad ways.

It certainly showed me that my addiction was a patient and crafty enemy. I would go through various convoluted mental gymnastics to justify what I was doing: I was not on the front line of crime any more. I was not harming anyone. A few times, I even believed what I was telling myself.

The morning of my release, 22 May 2006, came around. I had served six long years in various jails and now my life in the real world could begin again. So did I jump out of bed excited at the new possibilities that lay ahead of me?

No.

I turned over and went back to sleep.

I guess I knew I didn't have much waiting for me. My kids loved me, but now they were independent young people with lives of their own. I still felt I was doing the right thing going to Bournemouth, but I was far from thrilled by the prospect of dossing down in a probation hostel.

My psyche had now reached a weird point where when I was imprisoned I felt free. Release felt like I was being sentenced to another form of jail. I was exchanging a world that I knew for a world that I no longer understood, if I ever had done in the first place.

As I threw my worldly goods into a canvas bag, I reflected that I had no home, virtually no money, and was about to head into a world that had little time for offenders and ex-cons like me. I didn't know if anybody would give me a chance – and could I blame them? Secretly, even I wondered if I was worth it.

Saying my last goodbyes in reception, I stepped out into the cold light of day as the gates clanged behind me. There was nobody waiting for me, but I knew there wouldn't be. My mum had wanted to come, but I had told her not to bother, as I would make my own way to Bournemouth.

Lost without my chains, I fought a strong, desperate urge to turn around, knock on the gates and ask them to let me back in. Instead, I allowed myself one last look at those gates and took a deep breath.

'This is it, Ray!'

Slowly I walked away to get a tube to Waterloo and from there catch a train to Bournemouth. There was certainly no Yellow Brick Road in front of me, but at that moment I felt like a weird fucking combination of the Tin Man who had no heart and the lion who had no courage.

How strange was this? I felt like I was being sentenced all over again, but this time the sentence was one of freedom.

HOME BY THE SEA

It's a two-and-a-half-hour train journey to Bournemouth and I rallied a bit on the way down. My head was spinning as I watched the countryside whizz past at a speed that I was not used to, but I have always been a fighter and gave myself a good talking-to.

I can make this work, I told myself. It will be OK.

I can be quite persuasive, plus I have always been prone to manic mood swings, and as I walked out of the station at the other end of the journey my spirits had lifted to a state of quiet elation. As I breathed the sweet sea air, it sank in: this was it! I was a free man! I could do whatever I wanted!

But only up to a point. There were still distinct limits to my freedom. Despite all the good rehab work I had done in jail, my reputation still went before me, and the Home Office had only given me my parole with a hefty list of conditions.

I was still considered a possible risk to the public with a serious danger that I might backslide. Consequently I had to liaise closely with my probation officer, attend a probation meeting every week and live at the hostel. If I wanted to stay out overnight, I would have to ask permission.

What's more, I was not allowed to travel to London without giving a minimum of forty-eight hours' notice to probation. This gave them the chance to notify the police in the area that I was travelling to, in case any major crimes were committed during my stay. I also had to agree to random drug testing at any time. If I breached any of those conditions, I would be banged up again.

To me this all seemed very over the top and I bristled inside at the unfairness and indignity of it. But the authorities will never let you fully escape your past, so I had to just tell myself that I had once been a seriously dangerous man with a string of firearms offences and I was still paying the price. In any case, what choice did I have but to agree to these constraints?

As I stood outside Bournemouth Station, the kid in me was dying to leg it straight down to the sea, but I had to check in and meet my probation officer as soon as I arrived. Once I located and walked into the probation office, I got introduced to Sue.

Sue had the difficult job of dealing with all the people like me who were subject to public protection constraints, but she clearly knew what she was doing and luckily I liked her right away. She was friendly enough and promised to support me in any way she could. However, she also warned me that she would have no hesitation in recalling me if I broke any of my conditions or she thought there was any prospect of me reoffending. She was clearly not going to take any shit.

I left her office with the best of intentions. Within thirty minutes I had broken one of my conditions already.

Reporting to the hostel, I checked in and was given the key to the small, cell-like room I had been allocated. I dumped my bag on the bed and cast my eye around what was supposed to be my new home.

I had one thought, and one thought only: 'Bollocks if you think I am staying here!'

Why was this? Logically, I was grateful for this fresh chance and for being given somewhere to stay. However, I was also seething with resentment. I was tired of being ordered around, and the hostel just felt too much like an extension of prison. Yeah – bollocks if they thought I was staying there!

Instead, I moved in with a scaffolder mate called Billy in his place in Southbourne on the outskirts of Bournemouth. I also had an emotional reunion with Biscuit, who was also homeless following Danny's death and who now moved back in with me. Maybe we could make this work.

The support workers who ran the hostel knew me pretty well and didn't grass me up to Sue. In fact, after a few weeks we played it by the book and I applied to be allowed to live away from the hostel.

My case was quite a convincing one. I was earning an honest wage as a scaffolder, attending AA twelve-step meetings and had not missed one probation appointment. On the surface, by my normal low standards, I had transformed into a model citizen.

Not that everyone saw it that way. The authorities have very long memories and not everybody was totally convinced by my rehabilitation. Two days after I had officially moved into Billy's place in Southbourne, I got home from the gym one evening and immediately spotted an unmarked police car sitting outside our house. It's the kind of thing that I tend to notice.

The two coppers in suits sitting inside beckoned me over. They were polite and pleasant enough, but their message was clear: they knew who I was, they knew where I lived, and they were keeping a very close eye on me. Bournemouth was a quiet, law-abiding town and they wanted it kept that way.

Clearly somebody or other from the authorities had tipped them off that they had a psycho in their midst who was at major risk of reoffending, but I played it straight. I assured them that I was a changed man and they'd have no trouble from me. They replied that they hoped that was the case, and if it was they would leave me alone. Then they slowly drove off.

I found this encounter quite unnerving but also oddly reassuring, as I genuinely was still keen to avoid reverting to a life of crime. However, I had started off in Bournemouth living a lie as regards the hostel. Maybe my moral foundation wasn't quite as strong as I'd figured it was.

There is a wise saying that if you want to know where you are you should look at the company you keep. For all of my good intentions, I had still not let go of my villain image and mentality. When you are thinking and behaving that way, you attract a similar type of person, as sure as eggs is eggs. Water finds its own level.

As I grew into my new routine in Bournemouth, I wasn't actually doing anything wrong but I was still associating with ex-cons, thieves and dealers – the sort of people who had been my social circle my entire life. Old habits die hard. We all enabled one another and validated each other's bullshit on a regular basis.

This mentality is one of the hardest things of all to shake off. I came from a criminal world governed by rules of loyalty and trust that have to be earned. As a result I would rarely let outsiders in. It was so much easier to stick with my own people: my own kind.

I was feeling restless, uneasy and lonely in the outside world and had a definite feeling that there was a dark cloud on the horizon. Call it a self-fulfilling prophecy but these premonitions usually come true for me, and eventually my frustrations came to the fore in a twelve-step meeting.

After I had talked a bit about my time in prison, and told the group how I had escaped, another bloke in the group looked at me and said, 'I don't believe a word you are saying – it is all bollocks!' The red mist descended, and as we all stood up at the end of the meeting I smacked him one.

This was no way to behave in recovery, and that night I

felt ridiculous, stupid and most of all deeply inadequate. I had known my pride and ego had me heading for a fall and I had done nothing about it.

My anger could often scare me. It would come from nowhere and be savage, cunning and dangerous. Therapy had helped me to gain insight and to learn that so much of it dated from my troubled and bullied childhood, but this still didn't mean that I could always control it.

Also, I had been slogging along to the twelve-step programme meetings because they were one of my probation conditions but I had not been getting anything out of them. My short attention span and arrogance had led me to decide they were pointless and boring, and that resentment was what had led me to lash out and chin the bloke.

Luckily, because my mates had pulled me off the guy before I could do any more damage, the people who ran the meetings gave me another chance and didn't tell Sue what I had done. I was also to have another hefty, very undeserved stroke of luck when the last thing that I had ever expected happened at another meeting.

I fell in love.

Sam was a beautiful Mediterranean-looking woman whom I clocked as soon as she turned up at a meeting. For all of my front and bravado, I have always been very shy and awkward around attractive women. I suppose it makes sense: there is always the danger of rejection, the emotion which I am very used to and yet still the one that I hate the most. Recovering addicts are also strongly advised not to form personal relationships with other members of the group, but of course I wasn't going to let a little detail like that stop me.

It must have been something special when I met Sam because I found the courage to take a deep breath and offer her a lift home from the meeting as it was raining. A sensible woman, she vetted me with the other people in the meeting before accepting. I think it is safe to say, if she had got a full CRB check on me, she might have changed her mind!

I drove Sam to her home in Christchurch and as I dropped her off I asked for her phone number. She thanked me for the lift but explained that she did not give her number out to men unless she knew them. OK, that's that, I thought – until she asked if I would like to go in for a coffee.

I immediately realised that Sam was a very together person. She had a good stable job in a treatment centre and her home was immaculate, as was she. But as we sat and chatted about various things, I made her laugh and we appeared to get on well from the start.

When it came time for me to leave, I announced that I had lost my mobile phone and was expecting an important call – could Sam ring it for me? She did so, and it went off in my jacket pocket. Good – that was the phone number sorted, then. I drove home feeling mission accomplished.

That night I couldn't get Sam's beauty out of my head and I knew I had to see her again before the next meeting. Somehow I found the courage to invite her out – by text message. What a romantic, right? Waiting for a reply for a couple of hours was torture. Pacing around and stressing out, I must have lost two stones and gained a few grey hairs before my phone finally pinged.

Yes! She had agreed to see me the following Friday night. A smile spread over my face. I could not have been happier, or more relieved.

The date did not get off to the best of starts as I stupidly arrived late to pick her up. A scaffolding job had run over and I had gone home to freshen up without phoning to say I'd be late. Sam was not amused and opened the door with a frown, but she still looked amazingly beautiful to me as I gabbled my apologies. Eventually, she accepted them.

I turned on the charm as I attempted to make up for my cock-up over dinner at a nice restaurant local to her. Again, we had a real rapport as we chatted and laughed our heads off. Sam told me lots about herself but I told her very little – understandably, I feared that if she knew too much about my past she would probably have run a mile. Even in her high heels. Luckily she had only attended the one twelve-step meeting with me (she was a former alcohol addict) so didn't know much about my past.

I didn't want the evening to end and was delighted when Sam agreed to go on to a club in Bournemouth. It was such a good night that it wasn't even spoiled when I went to the bar to get our soft drinks, tripped over a bar stool by our table and went arse-over-tit on the floor. I felt a right wanker, but had to see the funny side.

One of the many things that I didn't know at this point in my life was how to have a relationship. Until then I had been so immersed in the world of crime that any relationships were totally superficial. They were mostly just about sex and I certainly never let anyone get close to me.

I guess I had filled that void with drugs. They had served as a willing substitute for the intimacy I secretly craved, and had become both my lover and my friend. However, they had become more and more demanding, cheated on me and ruined me. Plus, we were separated, but were we really divorced? It was always going to be an acrimonious affair.

That summer of 2006 was one of the hottest on record and I sweltered every day as I continued my scaffolding work. One day the temperature hit 103 degrees. My workmate (and landlord) Billy and I were like mad dogs in the heat, and now and then our boss turned up to check on us on a job only to find us down the beach, having a swim. He would just shake his head and leave us to it. He thought we were lunatics but he knew we always got the job done.

After work I would go to a twelve-step meeting, head for the gym or, best of all, hang out with Sam. I still had not missed a probation meeting and Sue had no concerns or issues with me. Life was feeling great, and I was finally able to enjoy my freedom and the beauty of an English seaside summer.

After a few months of dating, Sam asked me if Biscuit and I would like to move in to live with her. I was delighted. We were getting on so well that it seemed totally the right thing to do.

Living with her absolutely amazed me. Sam cooked fantastic dinners, kept the place clean and ran the house in a chilled way but with military precision. It made me realise that I had never really lived in a normal way before. After I had moved out from my mum's, my life had just been a succession of squalid council flats or bedsits or, more frequently, a single cell in a prison.

Things were going incredibly well and, for once, life seemed to be working out and making a lot of sense. So, naturally, I subconsciously began to look for a way to fuck it up.

Surrounded by so much happy normality, I naturally began to seethe and twitch internally. The compulsive thought began to grow in me yet again that I was inadequate and inferior to everyone around me. My psyche began feverishly to sabotage this newfound contentment.

A voice whispered inside me: how could I be happy? Me? I didn't deserve it! I was a piece of shit! And, inevitably, my addiction began to take hold again.

Suddenly it was like all the good work I had done at Grendon had never happened and I was back in full impulsive, selfish, random mode. Without even thinking, I made a decision: I would do what I wanted when I wanted, and nobody could stop me. In that frame of mind it made every kind of sense to buy a BMW for me and Sam to drive around Bournemouth in, even though we really couldn't afford it.

It also made even more sense for me to go out and get hold of some steroids again. My thought process was no more complex than this: I hadn't had any for quite a while, and I deserved them. Sam protested vehemently about the way I was going but she was wasting her time. I had stopped listening and in my self-destructive haze I felt powerless to prevent the inevitable.

In no time I had stopped working on any sort of recovery programme and was more and more unhinged by the day. With a few years of being clean behind me, I now just blithely assumed that I would never lapse and use again. And obviously, as ever, the steroids didn't count.

How fucking wrong can one idiot be?

Shortly after I had started laying into the steroids again, Sam came home from work to find me lying on the settee in agony, covered in sweat. Taking one look at me, she drove me straight to Poole Hospital. To say the least, I was not in a good way.

I had injected steroids straight into my thigh muscle and my body's immune system had immediately attacked them, thinking that they were a virus. My muscle had swollen so much that it was pressing onto a main artery that ran down my leg and restricting the flow of blood around my body and to my heart.

The doctors at Poole took one look at me and rushed me straight through to surgery. Later, as I recovered, they told me that if they had not operated to relieve the pressure I would have died from either a stroke or a cardiac arrest. They – and Sam – had saved my life.

The permanent scar all up the inside of my left thigh now reminds me of that particular act of stupidity and that I must never go that way again. Incredibly grateful to Sam, I felt desperate to treat her well and to reciprocate the love that she, for some reason, felt for me. Unfortunately, I just wasn't able to do it.

Like I said, my relationship history was a car crash. Certainly I had no inkling what an honest, loving, equal relationship was. All my encounters to that point had basically been about me and my needs and desires, and this one was also in danger of falling into that old pattern.

It wasn't that I was always emotionally cold. I could be passionate – even loving – at times. Yet still my old-school macho mentality meant that I thought I had to protect and look after Sam physically and financially and that was it. I had no idea about looking after her emotional wellbeing.

As I retreated into myself, Sam simply said that I was a mystery to her. She couldn't figure me out, and why should she be able to? I hadn't got a fucking clue myself. Yet oddly enough, even while I was hurting her by being closed off, I felt that I was pretty much the perfect partner.

Inevitably, I started spiralling into a dark place. My default mode of anger and self-loathing was stopping me being truly close to Sam. I was finding my work boring and had lapsed from any kind of treatment programme. My inner world was getting smaller and smaller as I retreated back into my raging, criminal mindset.

It felt like something very bad was about to happen. It did.

One morning I left for work at 6.30 a.m. as usual. I had a nagging toothache and it pissed me off all day on the scaffold. It felt as if I had enough to worry about without this crap bugging me. Why me?

After work I dropped my mates off at home as usual. As I swung the steering wheel to head back to Christchurch and Sam, a thought dropped into my mind from nowhere. Or maybe it was an instinct. My toothache was so unbearable that I was going to do something about it right now.

I figured that no chemist would have anything strong enough to deal with the pain, and the idea of a dentist never even crossed my mind. The solution to my throbbing molar was obvious as fuck: I needed to get some Valium to sort out the ache, and get to a dealer to get out of my mind.

I knew plenty of dealers in Bournemouth, and the nearest one was happy to oblige. He had Valium plus prescription medicines such as codeine phosphate, and I indulged myself like a starving man. Let's face it, the body of an addict like me can't tell the difference between a pharmaceutical opiate and a bag of street smack, and it doesn't care.

I didn't give a thought to the consequences. Or if I did, I thought this: fuck the consequences.

It was the early hours of the morning when I got home to Sam, barely able to stand. Even through my druggy haze, I saw the pain and hurt in her eyes. She looked devastated. I was off my head, but the guilt and shame that I suddenly felt was enough to penetrate even that high.

The next morning my remorse and self-loathing were a million times worse. What the fuck had I done? Disgust permeated every fibre of my being. I had thrown away my years of being clean for the sake of a temper tantrum just because I had a toothache. I could not believe I had gone to that dealer's. What kind of loser was I?

I reassured Sam with all my heart that it had been a

one-off, and I could not have meant it more. In fact, my con-
trition was so genuine and so complete that I swore I would
be completely honest about my lapse and seek help from the
people who were there for me. That very morning, I set off to
Sue's office to confess what I had done to my probation officer
and do whatever was necessary to get back on track.

Sue saw me straight away and I told her what had happened and asked if she could arrange for me to have some
counselling. She said that she would look into it and said that
I should re-engage with the twelve-step programme I had
recently abandoned. She left the room once, but I thought
nothing of it. When I left, I shook Sue's hand and emphasised
that I would do anything she wanted.

After all, we could beat this together.

As I walked out of the probation building I saw a sea of
police officers waiting for me. My experience told me what
was coming. I thought of legging it, but where to? While I was
debating my options, a group of them ran over, jumped me
and wrestled me to the ground.

Normally I would fight them like a dog until I was in
the cuffs. I used to take arrests like that as a personal affront:
when I was younger, even a stop-and-search would leave the
cops having to call for back-up units. Not this time. The fight
had gone out of me, and I just lay crushed on the ground, the
officers' full weight on top of me.

I was beaten, dazed and confused and felt like crying, not
fighting. At that second, I had no fight left. In less than a minute the triumphant officers had the cuffs on me, had shoved

me into the back of a police car and we were speeding to the local police station.

When we got there, the conversation was brutal. The cops told me that now I was back on drugs, as they saw it, the probation service had told them that the danger of me reoffending was simply too great. For the sake of public safety, I was to be returned to prison to serve the remaining three years of my sentence.

So much for the probation service supporting me. To think that I had gone to Sue and confessed spontaneously exactly what I had done! What a mug I had been. So this was where being honest had got me.

That had been one fucking expensive toothache. In my mind I heard the sound that I feared the most: the noise of a cell door being closed behind me, and the world locked out once more.

DAZED
AND
CAGED

Eight months! I had lasted no more than eight months in the land of the living, and now I was to return to the land of the dead.

As I sat in the cells of Bournemouth police station, I felt like the most pathetic fuck-up of a human being on the planet. It was made worse as I knew that I had nobody to blame for my plight but myself. I was going back to prison, and this time it felt different from how it ever had before.

Throughout my life I had always viewed imprisonment pretty much as an occupational hazard. There had been times I had even been relieved to go inside. I'd had no life worth talking about outside prison walls, and at my bleakest I'd figured that society was better off without me in it anyway.

This time was different. Instead of a mere scummy existence, I had a life and one that I actually enjoyed – living with the woman that I loved, in a beautiful house by the sea, and for once gainfully employed. The thought of three more years in a concrete coffin was just too much to bear.

Most of all, I was heartbroken and horror-stricken at just how much this would hurt poor Sam. Apart from my kids and my long-suffering mum, normally nobody could care less when I went inside. Now I had somebody who loved me – and this was going to hurt her just as much as me.

After a sleepless night, the next morning I found myself back in handcuffs and in the dreaded but familiar environment of a sweatbox as I was escorted to HMP Exeter. As I stepped down into the prison's compound yard and felt the grey, depressing aura of a nick all around me, I could have howled in despair.

Another, equally familiar emotion was taking over from the deep-rooted sadness I was feeling now: anger. Normally when I went inside I knew that I was at least bang to rights. This time I had a huge sense of injustice. I had been turning my life around, I had not reoffended, I had only lapsed once, and I had immediately gone to the authorities to confess my sin and ask for help.

It was all so unfair, and I had one question and one question only: what the fuck was I doing here?

Inside the building, the reception officer formally told me that I was on a recall for breaching my parole conditions and I would have to wear prison clothing. He explained that this was because HMP Exeter had no laundry facilities for cons wanting to wear their own clothes. He passed me a shirt and a pair of jeans and told me to get changed in a cubicle.

I threw them straight back at him: 'Go fuck yourself!'

I didn't even care what happened next. I had got plenty of kickings off screws before, and if I got another one, so what? I was in so much pain that the bastards couldn't hurt me any more.

The reception officer took one look at my face and knew better than to give me any more orders or try to manhandle me. He got on the phone and asked a prison governor to come down to see me.

Most governors are wise old ex-screws who are very experienced at dealing with all sorts of prisoners. The guy who appeared at Exeter was from this mould and had the good sense to be reasonable and defuse the escalating tensions of the situation. Looking at the state I was in, he agreed to let me wear my own clothing that day as long as I promised to wear prison uniform as soon as I was settled.

It was a little victory and an olive branch of sorts, and so I nodded and agreed. As I was led to a single cell on B Wing, I had calmed down slightly but I knew the deeper anger and raging torment in my soul would take a long, long time to ease.

They did not know what they were dealing with here. But they were soon going to find out.

HMP Exeter felt like a fucking dungeon of despair. Prisons are always noisy places and I was well used to the constant racket of convicts yelling from their cell windows to each other, but down here in Devon it seemed like all country yokels that were banged up. I couldn't understand a fucking word that most of them were bawling.

Nor did I want to. As I sat with my rotting soul in my brick cage, I couldn't get out of my head the pained expression and shock on Sam's face when I had turned up on her doorstep out of my head.

Looking back now, I could clearly see all of the mistakes I had made in recent weeks as I pissed away my whole hard-won process of rehabilitation. The bad company I was hanging with; the steroids I was filling up with; the way I had got cocky and over-confident again. All along, Sam had been trying to stop me and help me, and I had just ignored her.

Because I always knew best, didn't I? Muggins here? Look what a success I had made of my life so far! I went over and over these sorry thoughts into the early hours until I finally drifted off to a restless sleep.

Clang!

The familiar metallic thud of a cell door opening woke me up and I was up from my bed in a shot. I had only one impulse: I had to call Sam and check she was OK. In a flash, I got dressed and agitatedly ran down the balcony to the prisoners' card phone.

Some con was already on it, talking slowly and at length in his stupid accent. Pacing and twitching behind him, I was getting more and more wound up as the bumpkin prick went on and on, presumably about his new combine harvester and getting tickets for the next Wurzels concert.

I had to hear my Sam's voice. Did this idiot really think that his dreary concerns were more important than that? After a couple of minutes, I snapped, tapped him on the shoulder and told him that if he didn't get off the fucking phone now, I would smash it over his head. He took one look at me and finished his call.

Sam picked up straight away and sounded like she hadn't got much more sleep than me. My heart skipped several beats as soon as I heard her voice, but it killed me when she started crying as we told one another how much we missed each other. She told me that she loved me, she would wait for me, and she would be up to see me as soon as it was allowed.

I just about held it together until we said goodbye. I even gently replaced the handset before looking around me. As I saw the warders gathering to serve breakfast I felt an anger in me that I could not contain. With the strength of a man who had been going to the gym and injecting way too many steroids for years, I ripped the phone off the wall and threw it at them.

Here we go! Alarms bells went off all round the nick and officers came running from all directions. There was a tense standoff for a few seconds until a senior screw took control of the situation.

'All right, calm down, Ray,' he told me. 'Don't make this any worse for yourself.'

It threw me that he had used my first name but it also had the desired effect. I had learned enough from my therapy at Grendon to identify my real anger here: my heartbreak at being away from Sam and my sense of injustice at being banged up again. It wasn't the screws' fault. My fight was not with them.

For once I went to the segregation unit unaided rather than fighting, kicking and screaming. The senior officer walked alongside me. As he locked me in the cell, he told me that he had been warned about me the day before and had read my security file off the prison computer.

The guy said that it was obvious that I could be a handful but he understood how I must be feeling, being there on a recall and the way it had happened. I got the distinct impression that he sympathised with me. He even gave me a bit of good advice about appealing to the Home Office, and I thanked him as he turned the key and left.

The next day I was up before another prison governor on a charge of damaging the prison phone. He was a lot younger than the governor who had talked me down in reception on my first day and clearly didn't have much clue how to deal with problem prisoners on a mission to self-destruct.

After telling me that he would not tolerate behaviour like smashing up prison property, he told me that my punishment would be loss of earnings. This would mean that I wouldn't be able to buy another phone card to ring Sam, and I explained that was all I had to keep me going in there. He just looked up, waved away my comment and wouldn't even let me make one last call to her to explain.

Bad move, pal.

As I was escorted out of his office at the end of my hearing, I noticed that block's phone on the wall near to his door.

Before the officers could stop me, I ran over to the phone, wrenched it off the wall and threw it through the governor's window, sending glass flying everywhere.

There was a strange explosion in my head. Blackout.

When I woke up, I was sprawled in my cell with a hideous ache in my head like the worst hangover ever. I tentatively raised my fingers to the top of my skull and felt a sticky pool of lukewarm congealed blood. One of the screws must have smashed me over the head with his wooden truncheon, knocking me out.

Now I was fuming and I wanted to fight them. All of them.

When I am angry I get very, very unpredictable, and one thing I had learned in therapy was that I had to calm down before I got extremely violent. I knew that a fag would help, and I yelled through my cell door to the block orderly that I needed a cigarette.

Block orderlies are inmates who work in the segregation unit, doing menial jobs like cleaning and serving food. In my experience most of them tend to be rats and this one was no exception. He looked like a musclehead who thought that he was really something. When I asked him for a roll-up, he just replied that he wasn't allowed to give me one, and laughed.

This infuriated me even further as I am made of a different moral fibre. I was always a con's con who would stand firm with my fellow prisoners in their moment of need. I calmly said, 'OK, mate', but mentally I marked him down for some future attention.

That evening, when I was let out of my cell for dinner, I had no intention of eating a thing. Even so, I calmly walked up to the hotplate, well aware that all the officers around were watching my every move like hawks.

The same orderly who had refused me a fag was serving up the food and I could tell by his demeanour that he was trying to look menacing as he saw me coming. It didn't work. As he passed me a plate full of grey prison slop, I clenched my fist, leaned across the hotplate and gave him my best right hook to the jaw.

He went down, and so did I as a gaggle of prison warders ran over, leapt on me and pinned me to the floor. This time there was no civilised stroll to segregation. Instead, a gang of them bundled me back to my cell, threw me in and locked me up to calm down. No slop for me, then.

After a couple of hours an officer came to my door and asked if I had calmed down yet. I was in no mood for talking and so totally ignored him. 'Suit yourself!' he said and left, leaving what looked like a cup of tea behind for me.

I had had no fluid for hours and had nothing else in my cell so I picked up the tea, drank it and lay on my bed. When I got up for a piss a while later, I felt wobbly on my feet and could hardly walk. I knew at once what they had done, and thought to myself: 'You bastards!'

Although the authorities claim that they never slip prisoners a Mickey Finn or drug them against their knowledge or consent, the truth is that it goes on a lot. In recent years an enquiry has taken place and compensation has been handed out to prisoners for exactly this. It was not the first time it had been done to me and I had seen it happen to others. It's just one more thing that goes on within these walls that the outside world doesn't know about.

The following day I was back up before the same governor to face my charges of attacking the orderly and serial damage of prison telephones. I wasn't popular with him. However, I think a more experienced governor might have had a word with him as this time he was a bit more conciliatory and actually listened to me.

He proposed a solution: if he gave me a phone card, would I calm down and refrain from smashing up the prison? I said yes: all that I wanted was to be able to call Sam to make sure that she was OK. The governor told me that as long as I behaved I would be allowed to make one phone call a day to her.

However, he added that I would be kept in segregation for the good order and discipline of the jail, and I was also going to be transferred out of Exeter as soon as a space in another prison came up as they were not geared up to deal with the needs of long-term prisoners like me. He also gave me a two weeks' loss of canteen for decking the orderly. I couldn't care less about those things and went back to my cell without a fuss.

I was getting used to prison routine again but I hated every second of it. I missed my mum and my kids, I missed my job and my workmates, and most of all I missed Sam and Biscuit and our cosy little home. I was a ticking timebomb of rage and frustration that could go off at any minute.

Sam came in to see me, and she was a sight for sore eyes, but our time together was way too short and after she left I was even more bitter and resentful. So much of my life I had deserved all the punishment I got. This time, I knew I didn't.

After another two weeks in the Exeter segregation unit, I was transferred to HMP Guys Marsh in Shaftesbury, Dorset. Things got no better for me there, nor did I try to make them. As soon as I got out of the van at the jail I refused to wear their poxy prison uniform again, which meant that I was placed straight on to basic regime with no privileges.

Basic regime meant shit like I always got fed last at dinner, when the food was normally cold and tasted even more like dregs than usual. It was inedible, and eventually one day I piled as much slop on my plate as I could and hurled it at the officers and orderlies behind the hotplate.

Segregation unit again for Bishop …

I made it my business not to do a single thing that a warder asked me to do. I also developed selective hearing. If they called me from a way away, I totally ignored them until they came right up and in my face. If they told me to work, I would go straight to my cell and lie down. I was so jaded and angry that I was a constant thorn in their side.

It helped a bit – but not much – that I had a few good London lads locked up with me. Johnny James and his mate Dec were both south London boys like me and we hung around a bit on the rare times that I wasn't in segregation.

Johnny James is one of the gamest fuckers I have ever met. He was a prolific armed robber whose speciality was relieving jewellers of their valuables. His body was covered in scars from the many street battles he had been part of and I had never seen him back down from anybody. So when Johnny James called me a crazy fuck in Guys Marsh, I knew that something really *was* wrong.

There again, I supposed that people had seen me the same way over the years. I never set out to gain a reputation as a total lunatic but it has seemed to happen anyway. I suppose that I earned it, if that is the right word. It has certainly followed me through my life like a bad smell and even invited confrontations on more than one occasion.

I was in such mental anguish being away from Sam in Guys Marsh that I instinctively thought of getting hold of something to block it out. I had enough sense at least not to get into the shady drugs that were knocking around the jail, and so I went to the healthcare office to ask for something.

The prison doctor who I saw didn't seem that interested in my plight and wasn't really listening to me. He tried to palm me off with an anti-depressant that had made me feel ill when I had taken it before, and when I rejected it he said that he couldn't do anything else for me. So I decided to do something for him instead.

On my way out of the healthcare unit, I picked up a fire extinguisher and one by one smashed all the windows in the waiting room. Then I calmly walked back to my cell, packed my few small possessions and waited for the inevitable. It came: the familiar setting of a segregation unit and my name on the end of prison charge sheet.

Luckily for me, the governor at Guys Marsh was as sound as a pound. It turned out that he was once a prison officer at a young offenders' institution that I had been in as a kid for a while. He even remembered me, although obviously we had both aged a bit since then.

The governor was sympathetic to my grievance with the doctor in healthcare and so only gave me a week's loss of privileges. However, he had no choice but to place me on good order and discipline again, which meant that I would be kept in the segregation block until the authorities decided otherwise.

What happened next was a turning point for me in my ongoing battle with the people who were keeping me locked up. Punished with a loss of privileges, I had no tobacco and no phone card to speak to Sam. Neither was I able to get any. Obviously, my macho pride would not allow me to ask for any special treatment. I figured I would just have to lump it. And it hurt like fuck because Sam was my rock.

One morning I was doing my usual segregation-cell routine of a bit of exercise and shadow boxing when a few prison officers opened my door. I readied myself for action but I could see from their faces that they were not there to do me over. They placed a large brown bag on the floor, said, 'Courtesy of the governor!' and left.

I picked up the bag up and looked in it. It was stuff like tobacco and a few bits and bobs from the prison canteen. It might not sound much but to me it was momentous. Here I was in a segregation unit for an act of destruction, and I was being treated with kindness and respect. It threw me, to say the least.

The simple act by the governor of showing that he cared about me enough as a human being to give me a few small items touched me. It took the fight out of me – how could I be venomous towards such an act of humanity? To me, this was such a big deal.

It turned out that Sam had phoned the governor and had a lengthy conversation with him about me. She had explained all the progress I had been making in Bournemouth and tried to suggest a few ways to get me out of my confrontational, fucked-up mindset in Guys Marsh. They had come up with this brainwave of the gift between them.

It was a stroke of genius as it disarmed my futile rage and made me far more disposed to listen to the governor and take his suggestions seriously. I was very receptive when he suggested that I should transfer to a Rehabilitation for Addicted Prisoners Trust (RAPt) unit at HMP Coldingley near Woking in Surrey.

I went along with this plan, and three weeks later, to my delight, was transferred along with Johnny James and Dec. As we walked into Coldingley, it felt like a home from home (at least, as far as being in prison went). Immediately I was back around many of the London faces that I had been banged up with several times before.

In Coldingley I finally began to accept that I was back in prison and my campaign of non-cooperation, damage and violence was only harming me. I was accepted onto a twelve-week programme on the RAPt unit which was intended to further explore my addiction and see where it had all recently gone so wrong.

The counsellors Nick and Ally were absolutely fantastic, I liked the lads who were doing the RAPt treatment with me, and for the first time in weeks I found myself actually smiling and laughing again. It was time, finally, to pull myself out of my slump. The RAPt programme was a fantastic, independent unit of the prison services and I felt the counsellors on it actually cared.

Even better, the senior officer in the gym knew me from my amateur boxing days and encouraged me to get fit again. He brought in a skipping rope from home – against protocol, another act of kindness – and I would skip for hours. I also started circuit training with a mate, David Fraser, another ex-boxer who has kept himself as fit as a fiddle. David's dad is a bit of a legend in London's criminal underworld: 'Mad' Frankie Fraser.

My day would always start with a pre-breakfast phone call to Sam, which would leave me still missing her but on a high from at least hearing her voice. However, one day I rang but could tell right away that something was wrong. She was just too quiet, and then started crying as she told me that Biscuit had died. It slaughtered me.

I might once have been a vicious hard case and Britain's most wanted man and all that bollocks, but I was close to tears as I stood on that Surrey prison landing and heard that little creature was gone. A big hardened criminal stifling sobs over a dead budgie? You had better believe it. He meant everything to me.

Biscuit never was 'just a budgie' to me. I had raised him since he was a chick and the two of us had been through so much together. We had been caged for years. He had seen me at my worst, seen me fighting back in Grendon, and had enjoyed happiness with Sam and me.

He had known everything about me and I'm not ashamed to say that I loved that little creature with all my heart. In a funny way, he had represented an aspect of me that had been lost many years ago: the soft and gentle side that had been beaten out of me as a kid. By being so vulnerable, he had helped me develop my kind and caring side.

Biscuit had made my often-wretched life a bit happier. But I knew Sam would do right by him, and she buried him in a little pot and planted a yellow flower on top. It was the least that brave little bird deserved. Every year the most beautiful yellow flowers appear to remind the world of the beauty that was Biscuit.

Five months into my time in jail came the day of my appeal against my recall to be heard by a Home Office-appointed judge. I could not have been more nervous as I stood before him representing myself. I was up against the probation service and their selection of damaging prison reports since my recall. Talk about David versus Goliath!

The probation service went first with their argument that I remained a danger to the public and needed to be kept locked up. As I listened to them reading from reports from Exeter and elsewhere I cringed. On paper I sounded like a psychopathic monster. Sure, I had done bad things there, but I wasn't the ogre they were making me sound. It takes two to tango, and much of my fight had been the result of provocation.

The probation service claimed that as a former Category-A inmate with a history of firearms use and violence, I simply posed too much of a danger to society at large to be handed back to them to deal with. They acknowledged that I was on the RAPt course, but argued that my lapse in Bournemouth had shown that I was still likely to return to drug abuse and serious crime. They failed to give me credit for working and having a solid relationship and a home for the first time in my life. These fuckers really did *not* want me out.

When they had done, the judge asked me whether there was anything that I would like to say in my defence. This was it – my one and only chance. It was now or never.

Speaking without notes, I addressed the judge directly from the heart. As I spoke, I could see him listening intently to what I was saying. I started by admitting that my past, both long-term and recent, did not look good in any way, shape or form. I was not passing blame on anyone for my behaviour. I had messed up in many ways, and I held my hands up.

However, I went on to add that I had gone to every effort and then some to change my character and my flawed ways during my long period in prison. I had volunteered to go to HMP Grendon, I had put myself through rehab programmes and I had built myself a happy, sober life outside until that one fateful night.

Going on the attack, I explained that I felt very failed by the probation service. During the six years that I had served to date of my ten-year sentence, this public body that was supposed to assist and support me had not once visited me.

When I was released, they had done nothing to help me to reacclimatise to life on the outside.

On the only occasion that I had actually asked the probation service for assistance, when I had gone to them totally off my own bat to confess what I had stupidly done, they had not tried to understand and had instantly recalled me to prison. How could this be helping? How could it be fair?

I finished off by pointing out to the judge that at the time of my recall, for the first time in my life I had had a job, a good home and a loving partner. I stressed that technically I had not reoffended, I had not harmed anyone, and I had turned myself in when I didn't need to.

I had been doing my best and I had made one mistake. What else could I say?

The judge had listened intently but gave nothing away of his thoughts and feelings as he thanked me for my contribution and said the Home Office would let me know their decision in due course. I returned to my cell feeling that I had at least given the best, most honest account of myself that I was able. It was out of my hands now, and in the lap of the gods.

What did I think would happen? I really didn't know. But I prayed again to that God that I didn't understand and wasn't sure that I really believed in. I went back and forth but somehow, on my better days, I had this strange feeling that things might just be OK.

Three weeks had passed when a message rang out over the jail's tannoy system: 'Ray Bishop to the main office, please!' It could only be one thing.

When I got there, a senior officer with a stern and foreboding look on his face didn't say a word as he passed me a copy of a memo that he had received from the Home Office. My heart was in my mouth; time seemed to stand still as I opened the folded piece of paper and began to read from it.

The memo said that the reasons for my recall to prison had been unjustified and instead I should have been given the same chances of working through my problems as anyone else in the community. It added that although I had admitted one instance of drug use, I had asked the probation service for help immediately afterwards and not committed any further criminal offence.

Consequently, the Home Office was recommending my release from prison.

I was still gasping and grasping to take this all in as I looked up from the most precious piece of paper I had ever held and saw a room full of prison officers, all with broad smiles on their faces. They had known all along, and their boss had deliberately handed me the report with a sombre face so it would heighten my joy when I discovered the glorious truth.

They all shook my hand and my eyes welled up with tears of joy but there was only one person that I wanted to talk to right now. My beautiful Sam had been waiting for me for seven months and in a weird way had been caged just as I had. I needed to tell her that I was coming home.

I have to admit that I played the same dirty trick on Sam that the screws had pulled on me as she answered the phone.

Steadying myself, I just said in a deadpan, flat voice that I had heard from the Home Office, giving nothing away. The gulp at the other end of the line told me that she was beside herself with nerves, so I put her out of her misery:

'I'm coming home!'

Sam let out a shriek of excitement and burst into tears. At last we could both begin our precious life together again.

My release date was set for three weeks' time but I was not to have everything my way. For one thing, I was not to be allowed to go straight back to living with Sam. In light of my previous lapse, the terms of my release were that I was to stay in a hostel again, so that I could be regularly monitored and drug tested.

Obviously, I was not happy about this but I had no choice but to agree to the conditions. I had been down this road before and knew how to play it. The hostel I was going to was close to our home, so I would be able to spend most of my time with Sam as long as I slept in the hostel. In any case, it was a whole lot better than spending the next two years in jail!

When I told my mates on the wing the news they were over the moon for me. Mind you, I suspect that some of them may just have been glad to get shot of me, as I had been bending their ears and boring them stupid about Sam for months.

Even so, I was careful not to gloat about my good news. A favourite saying in prison is 'Time waits for no man' and I knew that some of my mates that I was leaving behind still had a lot of time to serve before they could take their own walk to freedom.

It was 5 May 2007 when I finally walked through the gates of HMP Coldingley for the last time. My RAPt counsellor Nick, who had become a friend as well as a helpful professional, saw me off the premises and gave me a farewell hug.

'You know what you have got to do, Ray,' he told me.

I nodded at him, because I knew that he meant I had to stick with the twelve-step programme, not go anywhere near drink or drugs and not even contemplate returning to a life of crime. I also nodded at him because I knew he was absolutely right.

I looked up and there, 20 feet away, stood my Sammy, staring at me with her arms wide open. Sprinting over to her, I picked her up and held her tight. I fell in love with her all over again, even though she was crying so much that her make-up had run and she looked like a panda. Through my own tears, I promised her that I would never do anything to jeapordise my freedom, and our happiness, again.

I meant it with all my heart. I had finally outgrown my cage and I was ready to fly.

WORK, STRESS AND PLAY

As soon as Sammy and I were together again we hit the ground running. It was brilliant – both exciting and fresh, and so good that it was as if I had never been away.

The fact I had lapsed and got banged up again could easily have killed a lesser relationship. The fact that we had stuck together during the hard times, spoken every day and come out of that dark period stronger clearly spoke volumes about just how much we meant to each other.

On my first day out we were so happy that we didn't know what to do with ourselves. We ended up going for a walk and feeding the swans and baby ducks in the river near our flat and then in the evening going for a curry in our favourite restaurant. We didn't care what we did as long as we did it together.

In the curry house, even as we talked as freely and happily as ever, I could sense Sam's doubts and fears. I had put this woman through hell over the last seven months, and I knew that she wouldn't be able to bear it if it were to happen again. So I held her hand and promised her that I would never go back inside again – no matter what.

I immediately started to attend twelve-step meetings again and was totally committed to staying drug-free. A good friend called Steve Mitchell volunteered to sponsor me through the recovery programme, which meant that he had been through the programme himself and would help to guide me through it. He has gone on to set up an amazing charity called the Silkworm Trust which feeds the homeless. They continue to support me to this day.

While I was going to the meetings I became very friendly with Gazza – ex-England footballer Paul Gascoigne. He was staying at a quasi-residential rehab centre in the town and going through a programme himself, and he and I hit it off straight away. He was a very down-to-earth, funny man.

The scumbag paparazzi had got wind that he was getting help in Bournemouth and harassed the poor sod everywhere he tried to go. So as well as being his mate I became his unofficial security man, getting him to and fro to his meetings away from the tabloids' prying cameras.

He was a lovely bloke and came round our place for dinner a few times. Sammy has no interest in football and had no idea who he was, apart from being a mate of mine called Paul.

He loved that: he told me afterwards it was the first time in years he'd been able to relax and not 'Be Gazza'.

I did not want to rush back to full-time work so I started to run a boxing club in my friend's gym twice a week. This helped me as it gave me something rewarding to focus on. People loved the sessions that we were running and before long it seemed a natural progression to open a gym of our own.

Along with two good friends, Roger Dorway and Stuart Maroney, we launched the R&R Boxing Academy Bournemouth. It is still going to this day, and whenever you see a fighter with an R&R top on, this is what they represent. I feel very proud of all the lads.

After a few months I also got the opportunity to start my own scaffold company with two friends, and I took it. After some deliberation we came up with the name Connex and starting advertising and doing business, which picked up at an amazing pace.

Just to keep things really busy, Sammy and I also moved into a flat above a café in Christchurch. The café was called Naughty Corner, and the deal was that Sam would run it for the landlord. Inevitably, she did an excellent job.

This was typical me, of course. A million miles an hour; trying to do everything at once; never saying no to anything. You've got to say yes to another excess. My feet hardly touched the ground each day. I felt like Sonic the fucking Hedgehog on speed.

With hindsight, it occurs to me that I had taken on way too much way too soon. I wish that it had occurred to me with foresight, instead. I had only been out of jail for a few months and I was still as crazy and frazzled as ever. What made me suddenly think I could be a multi-tasking business mogul? I think I was trying to play catch-up for all the wasted years.

Suddenly my days consisted of insane amounts of work. My nights meant going to the boxing gym, running it and doing some fighting. In the middle of all this, I was trying to have a relationship with Sam and do what was suggested for my recovery.

There are only so many hours in the day. Before long I found that I was constantly tired and always falling asleep. The scaffold business was growing at a rate that anyone would be proud of and I found it impossible to turn down jobs. In no time at all, Connex Scaffolding appeared to have amassed a fleet of five lorries and fourteen or fifteen employees.

You couldn't drive around Bournemouth without seeing our signs and we were taking on more and more and bigger and bigger contracts all the time. I could not have been prouder or more driven, but my partners and I were starting to find it incredibly stressful to hold everything together.

I was doing that thing again where I replaced my craving for drink and drugs with something equally all-consuming and extreme. Before, it had been working out. Now, I became a workaholic. Sammy could see the warning signs and had to tell me to slow down more than a few times. Once again, I thought I knew best.

I wasn't tempted to go anywhere near a pint or a joint, but nor was I fully focusing on my recovery as I had so little time to go to any twelve-step meetings. Most days I was held together by sheer exertion and willpower, and the strain was starting to tell.

In the midst of all this new pressure, my stress relief and solace was my boxing. Every time I stepped into the ring to spar with someone I loved it, as I felt it releasing something beautiful in me. Boxing gave me a thrill and adrenaline kick that nothing else in my newly sober life could equal.

I have had to accept that I am a strange man in many ways, and one of them is that I like taking punches as much as I enjoy dishing them out. Taking a good shot from a fighter makes me feel alive (although delivering one feels even better!). Why is this? I don't know, but it's what us fighters thrive on – why else would we get in the ring?

My training went up a notch one day in the gym when I met a mountain of a man named Big Jem Newman. Jem was once a formidable and major force in the London underworld but had since turned his life around and was now a respected nightclub owner in Bournemouth.

Over the years I had heard Jem's name mentioned many times, often in awe. I remembered that one time he had been convicted of shooting up a nightclub in Kingston-on-Thames over a dispute about doormen. It was a serious charge, and after a retrial he copped for a seven-and-a-half-year sentence.

Yet Jem really made his name when he controlled a lot of the doors in south-west London. Doormen are always hard bastards but even among them Jem was legendary as a strong enforcer.

When disputes arose he would be forced to fight, and he always took out whoever came against him, no matter how big or mental they were. Some of the guys that he beat in fair straighteners were notorious, yet Jem always stood head and shoulders above all of them.

Occasionally you meet people that you like so much and click so well with that you think you must have met them in a past life. Jem was like that for me and he immediately took me under his wing. He steered me back on track many times when I was in danger of faltering.

Jem's knowledge of boxing is second to none as he has been around the fight game his whole life. He had not only been a good boxer himself in his time, but also had the added quality of immense mental strength. When he began to train me, I realised that he understood a fighter's psyche like nobody I had ever met before.

Connex Scaffold still had more business than we knew what to do with but we were holding everything together until one of my two partners decided to go off on a mad cocaine binge. It left the other partner and me with no choice but to buy him out and get rid of him. This brought even more stress for the two of us as we carried more responsibility now.

It was all getting to be a bit of a struggle and once or twice I was tempted just to throw in the towel. At times it seemed like we were breaking our backs to keep the taxman happy (admittedly, a fairly new experience for me!). I am sure that anyone in business will understand when I say that he is the biggest bandit of all.

At least Sammy and I still had a good life together. The one thing that was missing for us was a child of our own. Sam had had a hysterectomy a couple of years earlier so couldn't have any more. She got on great with my two and had two cool grown-up sons of her own, Nick and Shaun, but they had both flown the nest.

I knew that Sammy had always wanted a daughter and I knew a way that we could get one. Unfortunately, my long criminal record meant that adopting or fostering were out of the question, but I produced the next best thing: a beautiful female Shih Tzu dog that we were to christen Poppy.

I had never seen Sam so happy as the day we collected Poppy. She fell in love with her instantly. They bonded like a mother and daughter from day one and Poppy was to become Sam's shadow. Sammy could not leave her sight for as much as a second without Poppy howling for her. Only a fool will go near Sam if Poppy is on her lap, as the fluffy little animal will happily eat you in bite-size chunks.

How protective is Poppy? One day in Lyme Regis she was wearing a little pink raincoat from a pet shop as we walked along. A large Alsatian dog approached Sammy and Poppy went mental at him, convinced that she was in danger. The big dog did not know what hit it as it was shredded by a tiny ball of fur in a pink raincoat. It beat a hasty retreat and is probably still in counselling to this day.

It was good that we had diversions like Poppy at home as at work my addictive nature was kicking in as badly as ever and I was becoming a worse and worse workaholic. By now my twelve-step programme had gone right out of the window. I had also got the boxing bug so badly that I decided I wanted to fight competitively again.

I contacted a promoter in Portsmouth who was the head of the WCBC boxing organisation. The WCBC had fighters registered all over Europe and put some great shows on so I applied to them for a boxing licence and was granted one after a medical.

Several other fighters from my gym got their licences at the same time and Roger and I set about managing them. The WCBC was the perfect forum to get our fighters matched up for shows.

In truth, our gym was growing in prestige as we now had a former world champion working as a trainer. Cornelius Carr had been WBA world super-middleweight champion in the nineties, a great era for boxing. We also had Joe Marino, an ex-US Air Force boxing champion, as a coach. Our gym was fast becoming the place for aspiring boxers to be.

Now we had Poppy, Sammy and I fancied moving from above the café so our new dog had a garden to play in rather than our shoe collections. We moved on from Christchurch to a beautiful new home overlooking the sea in the East Cliff area of Bournemouth. It was literally a stone's throw from the waves, and so many times I gazed from our windows and contrasted it with the bleak vistas I used to see from inside yet another segregation unit.

It was around now that I realised that, for the first time ever, I could look the world in the eye. I was free, happy, in a loving relationship, earning good money in business and being a useful and productive member of society. I was clean of both drugs and crime and even had a hobby that I loved, boxing. Compared to my miserable life to date, I was in heaven.

Doing good can be as addictive as fucking people over, and I made a point of devoting time to helping disadvantaged kids train at our gym. It was extremely rewarding and I think I helped a few of them. At least two of them have gone on to be very good boxers and gain a career in the fight game.

In mid-September 2008 I made my own boxing comeback after years in the wilderness at Portsmouth Guildhall. It was an epic night as loads of my friends and family came to offer their support for this unlikely comeback by a 35-year-old geezer.

On the day of the fight I was really nervous as I had not entered the ring as a fighter since I was a feckless youth. Any boxer who tells you that he does not get nervous is lying. It is a different kind of fight to one you might have on the street. Boxing is not about aggression and anger; it is all about skill and training.

Maybe my nerves got to me as I had a terrible first round. My opponent came out all guns blazing and I struggled to find my rhythm. I had just started to get into the fight in the second round when the referee stopped it to have a look at a cut above my opponent's eye. The ringside doctor said that he was unfit to continue and the fight was stopped.

The rules stated that if the fight was stopped due to an injury before the third round then it went to the judges' scorecards. Unluckily, I lost on points owing to the fact I had had such a slow first round.

That was disappointing, but the candle had been lit within my addictive soul as I felt a buzz like I had not felt in years. The adrenaline that pumped through my veins as I entered through the ropes felt amazing. I was definitely hooked and I could not wait to fight again.

Over the next six months I had another six fights and I won five of them as I was training even harder than ever. I was becoming pretty well known in boxing circles and the offers to fight on cards were coming in thick and fast. As ever, I just could not say no, and found myself in the ring more and more frequently.

Jem was still heavily involved in training me and described me as a peacock in a boxing gym. He said that when I came in I would always look stressed, but as soon as I stepped into the ring my feathers puffed up and I looked free. He was right – it is probably also the only place where I have ever really felt free.

I certainly wasn't feeling very free outside of it. From doing so well, the scaffolding business looked like it might be going tits-up. It wasn't even our fault. The banking crisis had driven Britain into recession, the credit crunch was biting hard and the building sector was particularly badly hit as banks stopped lending to developers.

Several building companies that we dealt with went into liquidation, as they could no longer meet their costs on ongoing projects. We had invoices out for nearly £200,000 but nobody was paying up. One after one we had to write the invoices off as firms went bankrupt.

It was an absolute nightmare. Rather than having any work scaffolding, I was spending my days trying to get in some of the money we were owed so I could keep the firm afloat. It was only black economy cash-in-hand work that kept us going.

I felt as though events were totally out of control and my stress levels were going through the roof. Sometimes I would wake up in the night shaking and covered in sweat. If I hadn't had the boxing to act as my stress relief, I would have been very tempted to turn back to drugs. Very tempted.

Sammy could see the effect it was all having on me and wanted me to give it all up, and Big Jem also told me that I should fuck the scaffolding off. The problem was that I felt trapped. We had worked so hard to build the firm up. It was my livelihood, and it was hard to walk away.

Things got even worse when my remaining partner got himself arrested in London for suspected money launder-ing. He got nicked in his Range Rover carrying more than £100,000 in cash and got locked up on remand.

This now meant that the entire running of the ailing firm fell on my shoulders. It might have looked from the outside as if I was doing well, as I was driving around in a Range Rover Sport, but the reality was it was a struggle to keep the firm afloat. I felt responsible for the employees, loads of whom had families to support.

Some people would have alleviated this pressure via yoga or Pilates. Being me, I hurled myself even further into boxing, using my frustrations and anger levels as an asset. I was in the gym every night and was in the best physical shape of my life, even if my mental state was increasingly dodgy.

I had a few underground fights on the unlicensed circuit as a way to relieve my stress. My match-ups were getting more competitive and I was beating better and better opponents. Eventually, the WCBC offered me the chance to fight for their British title at super-middleweight.

This really spurred me on and I became a man possessed. My training became psychotically intense, like a nutter Rocky Balboa with Big Jem as Uncle Paulie and Sam as Adrian. I spent hours and hours watching boxing DVDs and training with our ex-champs Cornelius and Joe. I sparred with any-body and everybody: lightweights, middleweights, heavy-weights. I think one day I even sparred with Poppy.

Leading up to the fight I had three warm-up bouts, win-ning them all by knockouts. Boxing never failed to lift my mood, especially as I was so good at it: I had a good fighter's brain and the heart of a lion. I just wished that I was equally talented in the other areas of my life.

The truth was that I was using boxing as a distraction from my failings in other areas. I was winning in the ring, but losing badly outside of it. I was on the ropes and I would not admit it to anyone, instead hiding behind my Range Rover and platinum Rolex.

But I remained an addict – and prestige and property are not enough to keep you clean. Even if, bizarrely, you are on the verge of becoming a British champion.

INTO THE RING

There have been so many moments in my life when I have absolutely loathed and despised myself and been sure that I would never amount to anything. It had certainly never crossed my mind that I might one day be the *crème da la crème*.

Having sanctioned me having a championship fight for their UK super-middleweight title, the WCBC got in touch with more details. I was to be up against a Portsmouth fighter named Frankie Brooks – and the bout was to be at the Pyramids Centre in his own backyard of Southsea.

This was a daunting prospect. Not particularly because of my opponent, who I didn't know a lot about, but because I would also be taking on his home crowd. You often find that when a fight goes to the judges' decision they tend to give it to the home fighter. Over the years I have witnessed some shocking verdicts for that very reason.

Even so I was determined to give it my best shot. For any fighter, a title fight is the ultimate dream. It is what you let yourself fantasise about during those long hours in the gym and punishing training and sparring sessions. Boxing is such a strict discipline that to be the best you have to go the extra mile.

In fact, I was so serious about this fight that I cut right down on the fags.

Even if I were tempted to slack, my team wouldn't have let me. Big Jem was my main motivator and corner man, and as well as working me hard physically he instilled belief in me. Joe Marino also put me through my paces, and being trained by a former US champion certainly kept me on my toes.

I tried to carry myself in the ring in the same way as people like Joe, which was like a proper classy fighter. Over the years I have noticed that true warriors are humble types who never give it the large. They come into a gym and are respectful and courteous to all. They are not flash because they have nothing to prove to anyone.

In my time I have lost count of the number of would-be hard men who walk into a gym like they own the place. The truth is, real fighters like me can spot these frauds a mile off. They usually tend to be bullies who pick on the weakest links and rarely step up to the plate against a proper boxer.

When I sparred with these pretenders, they would always come out of their corner like a rocket and try to take my head off in the first round. They had no concept of ringcraft and treated fighting like brawling, throwing themselves into each punch with no variation of power.

This would play into my gloves because skilled boxers use aggression from their opponent to their advantage. I would lure these bullies forward with soft punches until I saw an opening and then … bang! In the run-up to my title fight, I came up against a few of these chancers and taught them a lesson.

I had always managed not to get this cocky myself. In my up-and-down career I had won plenty of fights and lost plenty of others, and in some ways the losses were more important because they kept me grounded and humble. Once you start thinking you are the big 'I am' in the ring, you are riding for a fall.

Even so, outside of the ring things were still not going swimmingly for me. My work problems were getting worse and made me totally eschew recovery meetings, and even worse, despite all of my promises to her when I came out of jail, I was not being a good partner to Sam.

I was taking my work stress home and snapping at her for no reason and was giving less and less thought to what she needed from me, and from our relationship. For a while, I honestly think I was showing more affection to Poppy than I was her. She felt neglected, and rightly so.

My behaviour was all the worse as she was totally supportive of me in every way, both trying to keep the business afloat and getting ready for my fight. She didn't like me boxing – what woman likes seeing their man getting smashed around the head and body? – but she knew it was good for my state of mind so she bit her tongue.

I knew I was being unfair, so on the night before the bout I took Sammy out for a lovely meal and promised that after the fight I would be far less stressed. What happened next threw me. She held my hand, gave me her special loving smile, and told me that I was a beautiful man.

I have been called plenty of things in my life, but that was a first. It really touched me as I have always felt far more of a beast than a beauty. To be told such a nice thing by such a beautiful saint took my breath away. I felt undeserving, but very grateful.

That memorable evening had another high point. My mobile rang and I answered it to hear a strange accent that I didn't recognise at all.

'Hello, Ray, it's Joe,' the guy said.

'Joe who?'

'Joe Calzaghe.'

What an amazing moment! Big Jem has anybody who is anybody in boxing on speed dial, and had arranged for Joe Calzaghe, the Welsh former super-middleweight champion who used to get called the best pound-for-pound fighter in the world, to give me a call. I could hardly take it in.

Joe and I had a great chat and he gave me some sensible advice. He had been told that I was a banger but told me to take my time, go in there and box and wait for my opening. 'If you see your chance, then knock him out,' he concluded.

'What the fuck do you know about boxing, anyway?' I asked him. Luckily, he laughed.

On the morning of the fight the next day, I grabbed Poppy and went off for a long walk along the clifftops. It was a time for reflection. Gazing out over the Channel, I marvelled at just how much my life had changed for the better in the last few years.

In years gone by, having a fight for me would have meant a bar-room brawl because somebody had disrespected me, said something I didn't like or looked at me funny. When I used violence it was nasty and sometimes indiscriminate. Now it was legit, civilised and even admirable – and I actually pinched myself to make sure that I really was boxing for a British title later that day.

I had turned a corner, I no longer wanted to hurt anybody, and as I stood there on the clifftop I told myself that, if I were to win the title, it was for all the people whose lives I had damaged in my criminal career. They would never know it, of course, but in a weird way I was doing it for them.

I spent the rest of the morning trying to relax with Sam, but obviously the fight was playing on my mind. I had to be in Portsmouth at two in the afternoon for the weigh-in and a pre-fight interview, but then the fight wasn't until about nine at night. That was a fuck of a lot of time to kill.

Luckily I was travelling down mob-handed with Jem, Joe and a load of other fighters from the club. At least I would have plenty of supporters – and people who knew about boxing – around to help take my mind off it yet also keep me focused at the same time.

After getting on the scales – bang on my fighting weight – I got interviewed for Boxing Evolution TV. The blonde female interviewer didn't seem too up on boxing and might well have been betraying roots planted firmly in Essex as she hit me with her first question.

'Who are you playing tonight?'

'Chelsea,' I told her.

As least she gave me a good laugh, which was what I needed, as I was feeling pretty tense by then. My opponent, Frankie Brooks, weighed in and we had the usual macho stare-down thing that boxers go through before a fight. I could tell I was in for a tough night as he looked in really good condition.

I just hoped Frankie smoked as much as me.

My entourage and I headed out for a meal and then a quick drink – for them, anyway – before the fight. By now I was getting more and more apprehensive and the butterflies were kicking in big time. I was trying my best not to smoke at all before the fight, but ended up having to have a couple to steady my nerves.

I just wanted to get it over with, but back at the venue, as the doors opened and dozens of fight fans began to pour in, the atmosphere grew electric. My fears about fighting on my opponent's home turf were largely nullified, as it seemed like half of Bournemouth had travelled down to support me.

A lot of people had also made the trip down from London to cheer me on. In fact, I'd go so far as to say that the Metropolitan Police could take it easy that night because there were a lot of serious criminal faces in attendance. I was not used to having that many people in my corner – either in boxing or in life – and I found it all a little bit overwhelming.

A guy called Big Stevie Edwards came up to me and said, 'Win, lose or draw, you're a champ in our eyes.' This meant a lot coming from a face of his status and calibre. Steve had once been a fearsome operator on the notorious Cambridge Estate in Kingston-on-Thames. He was Big Jem's right-hand man for years but had turned his life around just like Jem had, and I looked up to him.

Many of the old guard who I had served time with in various prisons also showed up. My pal Johnny James was there, as was another good friend, Tony Baigo. Looking round at the sea of familiar faces, suddenly I had the feeling that this was going to be my night. I even began to feel sorry for Frankie Brooks, because I knew he was in for a hard evening.

Sitting backstage with Jem and Joe, I tried to chill out and relax. This was nigh on impossible as the evening had a very strong under-bill so I could hear the excited shouts and groans of the crowd in the arena. Sam came in looking like a million dollars and wished me luck, even though she and I both knew that she hated it every time I got in the ring.

My other trainer from the gym, Cornelius, came up to do my bandages and I got changed into my shorts and boots. Big Jem put my gloves on, and as soon as they were laced up my butterflies came flocking back. Looking at the gloves, I knew there was no turning back now.

I felt sharp as Joe warmed me up on the pads and Jem kept on telling me that I was the best and couldn't be beat at this weight. He was getting me ready for the lion's den. A couple more distinguished supporters dropped by: Roger

Dorway, the other R in R&R Boxing, who is also a formidable fighter, and Marcel Kelman, a regular sparring partner and a former European kick-boxing champion.

Then it was time. As the MC did his pre-fight announcement and bigged up our bout, I made my way through the arena.

On the long, lonely walk to the ring, you experience every emotion you can imagine, and a few more that you can't. Your heart is in your mouth and coldness runs through your veins. Sounds are muffled, and you struggle to pick out anyone's face in the crowd. Your legs feel so light that you could be on roller skates.

Eventually you climb through the ropes into what feels like the worst segregation unit ever, the loneliest place on earth, and – boom! It hits you! This is it!

Everything seems very real and not real at all. You can hear familiar voices but have no idea where they are coming from. Are they just in your head? Are you imagining this whole thing? Before a big fight, there are always a few seconds that are like an out-of-body experience.

Then you snap out of it. Get back in the room. Take a deep breath and check your surroundings. You focus on little things, like checking the ring for springiness. Boxing is all about footwork, and a springy ring makes it far easier to duck and weave in and out.

When Frankie and I stepped to the centre of the ring with our trainers, I realised what I was dealing with. Not only was he lean and in great shape, but his coach was Paul Dyer, a well-known former pro from Portsmouth. He was clearly no mug, and I was up against it.

The referee told us the normal stuff about wanting a clean fight with no holding or low blows and sent us back to our corners. I said a silent, private prayer to a God that I believed in rather more than usual at that second. OK. This was it.

Seconds out! Round one! Ding ding!

The bell rang and Frankie came flying straight at me and threw a great combination. I took the punches on my gloves but could feel at once just how powerful he was. I didn't want to get caught early doors, so I slipped and parried as he rained a series of heavy blows down on me.

At the start of a fight I always use my brain to work out what kind of fighter I am up against, and it was obvious Frankie was a very busy one. I took my time as I weighed him up, using stiff jabs to keep him back. It frustrated him and he got on the front foot and started to lunge in more.

I noticed that he was head hunting – throwing nearly every punch towards my head and not aiming much at my body. Just like Joe Calzaghe had said, I waited patiently and picked my moment. Slipping a blow, I placed a left hook into Frankie's rib cage and felt the wind go out of him as he dropped to one knee.

The referee began his count and I waited in a neutral corner, secretly hoping against hope that that was it. But Frankie was made of sterner stuff and came back at me even harder. We battled our way through five hard rounds where there was little to separate us.

As fighters tire, they make more mistakes. I began to notice that Frankie had started to over-extend his right arm when he threw it straight, and before the last round I came up with a plan. I would step to my left to try to lure him into throwing the punch, and I would throw a left hook straight over the top of it.

I didn't get a chance at first because he made one more effort and started the last round well, getting in a few good shots and leaving me feeling a bit dazed. It was now or never. I tapped deep into my inner resolve, pushed him away, threw a flurry of punches – and stepped to my left.

What was that the A-Team used to say? They loved it when a plan came together? Frankie threw a right and I saw my chance almost in slow motion. As the punch came towards me, I sidestepped it and put everything I had into a left hook. It smacked Frankie on the jaw and his head hit the canvas.

The referee counted up to eight and I was not expecting him to get up at all. But Frankie Brooks was the comeback king and amazingly there he was in front of me again, throwing big bombs. When the bell clanged for the end of the fight we both raised our hands to claim victory.

The crowd went mental because they knew they had seen an epic battle. Frankie and I collapsed into one another and hugged – it was the only thing keeping us both upright. As we separated and staggered back to our corners we could only wait for the judges' verdict.

I asked Jem and Joe what they thought and they said it could go either way. I hoped that putting him on the canvas twice would go in my favour, but I knew from some bitter past experience that this was no guarantee – plus, of course, we were in front of Frankie's home crowd. I thought the most likely outcome was they would call it a draw.

After a few very long minutes, the ref called Frankie and me to the centre of the ring for the MC to announce the result. He took the mic.

'Ladies and gentlemen, we have a unanimous decision. Your winner in the blue corner, and also the new WCBC British Champion … Ray Bishop!'

The second that I heard my name called, I fell to one knee. I was overcome by emotion. I felt like my whole life had been leading to this moment. My mind flashed back to the poor, bullied kid, always made to feel weak and inferior, who was now standing vindicated, a champion boxer.

Was it really happening?

As if in a dream, I consoled Frankie, who congratulated me like the gent and true fighter he is. The president of the WCBC appeared in the ring, placed a belt around my waist and raised my hand. If this was a dream, I didn't want it ever to end.

I could hardly hear myself think for the cheers and yells of the crowd, but after a few photos I stepped out of the ring and made my way through the well-wishers. There was only one face I desperately needed to see and that was my gorgeous Sammy, who had always given me everything. I put the belt on her and kissed her.

Amid all of the acclaim and the congratulations, only one thing really mattered to me – that she was proud of me.

DOWN FOR THE COUNT

The euphoria from my title win lasted for quite a few days, then slowly but surely real life began to kick back in. I had to get back to reality – and my reality was not looking good.

Things were going from bad to worse for Connex Scaffolding. The winter months are always the worst time for the building trade, and with the British economy still in a slump the winter of 2010 was brutal. There were not enough jobs to go round and we were competing against outfits that were literally buying the work. They were smaller firms than us without our overheads.

We had no choice but to downscale. I hated doing it but I couldn't justify having so many men on the books any more. It killed me having to lay them off, as I was aware they all had families and would be in difficulties. We also had to cut back to just two lorries.

The rent on our yard was quite high so we moved to try to save some money there. We managed to get new premises that we leased from the Coopers, a well-known travelling family in Dorset. They were also synonymous with boxing – Gary Cooper had even been a British champion and trains up-and-coming fighters nowadays.

His brother, Charlie, gave us an excellent yard right next to a stock-car racing track so now we had to move all of our equipment to this new base. Ideally, scaffold firms move in the summer, when they have plenty of stuff on, most of the tubes and boards are already in use, and they can move stuff to the new yard as they finish each job.

Connex didn't have that luxury. We had hardly any work on apart from unpaid labour taking the old scaffolding down from previous jobs, and so had literally thousands of boards and fittings in our yard, not to mention tons and tons of tubes to move. It was a mammoth task, and we had no choice but to do it every evening after we had finished work.

It was an inhuman schedule, and during the month that we were doing the move I was getting more and more fucked. I even began to look ill and Sam was getting really worried about me. To be honest, so was I. I really needed a holiday in the sun, but as I had been banned from holding a passport for ten years, this was not an option.

Sammy had gone to Cyprus without me a few times as I insisted she shouldn't have to suffer because I couldn't travel.

It did mean, though, that the only release from the stress that was doing my fucking head in was the gym.

At this point I was taking a break from fighting but a lot of the gym fighters were still active. I trained and cornered a lot of them. A few very tough Russian fighters joined and came to train with us. They were like machines in the gym and had no off button: they just kept going until we closed for the night.

Consequently R&R was becoming a really well-respected stable and we had some great victories up and down the country. I was proud of this, but I was so distracted and under so much pressure from the other things in my life that I couldn't fully enjoy our success.

Inevitably, the stress in my life was also causing cracks to appear in my relationship with Sammy – serious cracks. I was growing so resentful of my situation and my life in general that I was not good to be around. I was going to no meetings at all, giving my recovery no thought whatsoever, and hanging on to sobriety by a thread.

This thread was to snap.

As my mental state got worse and worse, I started taking Valium to cope and to help me sleep. I justified this to myself as I had been given a prescription for it by a doctor, and that was what normal people did, right? What I was forgetting, or choosing to ignore, was that I am not a normal person where drugs are concerned – I am an addict.

Most people can use tranquillisers as a crutch for a while if they are going through a hard time, but they are a luxury that I just cannot afford. As soon as I started taking them it was obvious that they would trigger fond memories of other drugs – and now I was not engaging with meetings and recovery, what was to stop me?

At this point my business partner was released from prison and the situation changed dramatically. While he was inside, he had made me a series of promises with regard to Connex. He held the controlling stake in the company, but had agreed to sign over an extra percentage to me and another manager who had worked alongside me.

When he came out it became clear that he had no intention of going through with this. I had been totally loyal and done right by him while he was inside, so this change of mind really stung me. I felt hurt, used and abused, and at that moment I gave up trying to save the company.

I walked away from Connex with nothing, as my partner technically owned all the assets as large loans had been secured in his name. After the company had been broken up and sold and all of our debts paid back, there was not a lot left to go around.

It made me realise that I had worked my arse off for the last three years for absolutely sod-all. Yet I have no doubt in my mind that we could have salvaged it between us if we had communicated more. Still, I don't bear my old partner any malice whatsoever. He is a good man and I guess we just lost our way a bit and couldn't see the wood for the trees. Both of us were also fighters who hated to surrender.

Of course the end of Connex brought fresh pressures. I

still had to earn a living and felt lucky to get a few job offers from other scaffolding companies. The problem was that these firms were in the same predicament that Connex had been in, meaning that we had to work extremely long hours to ensure that we kept limping on.

The pressure remained relentless. I would regularly leave the house for work at five in the morning and not get back in until around eight at night. Physically, I was running myself into the ground; mentally, I was struggling to cope.

Things couldn't go on that way, and they came to a head one day as I was dismantling a scaffold at AFC Bournemouth football stadium. One second I was standing on a board: the next thing I knew, I was falling through the air. I had enough time to think on my way down, and what I thought was this: 'This is going to hurt.'

I fell more than 20 feet, which is like falling off the roof of a house, but fortunately landed on some gravel rather than the stretch of concrete next to it. Even so, I landed on my back and straight away felt a searing pain in my side and my left wrist, as well as being badly winded.

It says a lot about my sorry mental state at the time that my first thought was that I had broken my back – and yet I immediately jumped up and tried to get back on the scaffold to carry on working. All I could think about was that I had to work to pay our bills, and that seemed far more important than whatever injuries I might have picked up.

Luckily, my boss was rather more rational and carted me off to hospital, complaining as I went. It turned out that I had broken two ribs and also fractured my wrist in three places. This filled me with dread. Sammy and I had been struggling to pay our bills already, without this latest fucking disaster.

I was tying myself in mental knots. Sam and I had not been going well because I was in turmoil about work, and somehow in my mind I thought that everything would collapse if I was unable to work and earn a living. Now, I couldn't. Sitting in a hospital bed, I felt as if all hope had gone.

Mixed in with this was a fear that if I couldn't work legally I would automatically revert to being a criminal. I hated the fact that I had lived that way for so much of my life, and I desperately did not want to start doing so again. I would have cut my arm off not to do that – and I almost did so, literally.

My arm should have been in plaster for a month at the very least, but after just a week I cut the plaster off with a pair of huge industrial scissors and went back to work. Even for me this was insanity, and the pain was so severe that I had taken to consuming opiate-based painkillers to get through the day. Now I really was on the slippery slope.

It was all too much for Sammy. She was simultaneously furious with me and incredibly frightened as she saw me pushing the self-destruct button yet again. I was turning into a complete nightmare to be around, and I came home from work one night to find she had taken Poppy and moved into her mum's place.

I didn't doubt that Sam loved me with all her heart but it is not a pretty sight to watch the person you love destroy himself. She was finding the pain too much to bear and she had to abandon ship. I understood completely – but I also knew that without Sammy's stabilising influence I really was in trouble.

At this point I reckon I quietly had a breakdown. I virtually withdrew from the world. Every morning I would get up, work all day and then return to our empty home and sit in our bedroom. It became my new prison cell: I rarely even ventured anywhere else in the house.

I could not bear being without Sam and Poppy in the space we had shared. I hated even catching a glimpse of the garden, with all the beautiful flowers that Sam had spent hours planting. I was a pretty sick puppy, and all I could do was to watch videos about the wonders of the universe repeatedly, as they were the only things that could distract me.

It made things even worse that my last remaining grandparent died at this time. My nan was my last surviving relative on my dad's side and she died on my birthday, just like my dad had done. It felt like the Bishop side of me had also died out – and what had I achieved? What had I ever done?

Naturally I took what had always been my natural escape route. I tried to numb my emotional world even more. I began going to chemists and buying boxes of codeine-based painkillers. I would take handfuls of them, trying to snuff out the physical and existential pain I was in.

It was an OK short-term solution but my pain was too deep and profound and would soon force its way through again. My solution was to increase the dose, plus gobble more Valium, and try to knock myself out to sleep any time that I was home.

I was in such a terrible condition that I did things that to any normal person would seem totally insane. One night I got in my car, drove all the way to London and parked right outside Latchmere House prison. My life had got so unbearable that I was desperately longing to be inside again, back where I felt safe and knew what the rules were.

It was the act of a man totally at the end of his tether, and the sad irony was that I couldn't go back inside even if I tried. My parole had ended a year ago so I was no longer on recall, and I was no longer mentally able to commit a fresh crime to get locked up. Serious criminality had been removed from my psyche.

As I realised that being a criminal was over for me, even though I felt that I belonged in jail, I sat in my car outside the prison and sobbed – for Sam, for me, for my lost and wretched life. I felt like the loneliest creature on the planet. I probably was.

Just when you think things can't get worse – they do. I got sicker, both physically and mentally, and was forced to stop working. With no money coming in, I lost the home that Sam and I had shared. It killed me and once again I felt like the biggest loser on the planet. Just what was the point of me?

I had no fight left and every breath I took was like a surrender. I simply did not care about myself any more and I deteriorated further every day. While I never went near any doctors, I'm virtually certain that I had a breakdown. I don't know what else you can call it.

With no one to care for and no one around to care for me, I went back on the drugs with a vengeance. I hunted them down like a caveman hunts food. People started to avoid me again, and I don't blame them, because I got pretty scary to be around, and very volatile.

In no time I owed money to plenty of dealers and was falling back into crime. Or, at least, trying to: I couldn't even get that right. I tried to steal from shops like I had done as a kid, but I've never been a good sneak thief, and just ended up getting into fights with security guards.

Despite my aversion to my old criminal lifestyle, I was right on the edge of going back to serious crime. The only thing that stopped me was that Big Jem and a few people from Narcotics Anonymous were looking out for me. They hated seeing how I was, and would give me money to try to stop me doing something stupid.

Sammy hadn't given up on me and while she could not handle living with me in the condition I was in, she also tried everything she could think of to get me back on track. But by now I was too far gone for even the woman I loved to reach me.

Sometimes you have to hit the bottom before you start to climb. In all my years of abusing drugs I had steered clear of injecting, but as I continued on my suicide mission I started letting dealers inject me with heroin. In fact, I would insist that they did it.

This period of my life was truly pathetic. I didn't know how to inject myself, and so would buy drugs and then trawl the streets looking for junkies who could shoot up into my arm for me. They would do it, of course. They'd do anything for a few notes or a bag of smack.

I couldn't go on this way for long without dying. I didn't.

In the early hours of one morning, I OD'd in a scummy crack house and was dumped on a street by a fellow druggie, who called an ambulance. My heart had stopped, but a passer-by who had knowledge of CPR managed to keep me going until the ambulance came.

It may sound crazy, but I believe that my life-saving Good Samaritan walking by was divine intervention. In the ambulance they told me that if my saviour had just put me into the recovery position, as most people would have done, I would have died. What were the odds of a man with that kind of specialist knowledge strolling Bournemouth's back streets at that time?

All in all, it had been a close shave. When I had fully come to, the medics wanted to keep me in hospital for a few days and run some tests on me.

I refused. I had a far better idea. I went back to the crack house …

THE END GAME

CHAPTER 21

So this was my life.

It was 2011. I was thirty-eight years old and a spiritual and mental wreck. The man who two years earlier had won a British boxing championship was now two stone under-weight, addicted to opiate painkillers and little more than a human pincushion. I felt like a piece of shit. I looked like it, too.

If I ever looked in a mirror, which I tried to do as little as possible, I saw track marks in my jugular vein from my intra-venous use. Most days I could not even get it together to feed myself, hence my emaciated and skeletal state.

I hated my home and it wasn't safe for me to be there any-way, as several drug dealers had separately decided it was time for me to start paying up for the many drugs I had 'borrowed' from them. It was the only way I could get what I wanted – I had no income at all, and had exhausted all other means of getting money. The way I was by now, I couldn't even have got a job cleaning cabins on the *Titanic*.

I have had some bad times in my life, but what was left of me knew that this was a new low. Most of my friends and family seemed to be avoiding me now. Sammy still loved me but she was staying away, knowing the pit I was in was so deep that even she couldn't help me out.

It was obvious to everyone, me included, that I was basically committing suicide, one fix at a time. With no restraints left, I was hitting rock bottom and carrying on digging. When I saw Christmas decorations going up everywhere, they were like a dagger in my heart as they emphasised just how alone I was.

I'm not exactly the sort of person who goes around quoting Shakespeare, but he once said that, 'All the world's a stage … And one man in his time plays many parts.' He could easily have been referring to addicts like me. Robbed of our script for life, we act our way through as if it is one big theatrical show. Our need for acceptance and approval is so deep that we will be whoever you want us to be.

Yet, as we don our masks, the stage where we play out our lives gradually grows ever lonelier and more desolate. There don't seem to be any other characters in our play. So naturally we become ostracised ourselves from the rest of humanity and hide deep in our own twisted minds.

Acting out the dramatic tragedy of my life had left me in so much agony that I was on the brink of taking my own life. In truth, I had begun to plot my suicide as my despair seemed total and impenetrable. If this was my life, I saw no point in living it any longer.

The human mind does some pretty weird stuff when it is pushed to extremes. In the nights after my OD, I had a series of bizarre dreams. Some were extraordinarily vivid, and in one in particular I was in a field surrounded by smiling, angelic figures, and suffused by peace and happiness.

It could not have been less like my grubby, pointless day-to-day life, but when I awoke I decided that before I killed myself I would have one more attempt at getting clean. I would go to my local drug support agency.

I made it there in the worst state imaginable. I was a bitter, defeated zombie. After I pressed on the intercom, and a voice came through the speaker system inviting me to enter, I spent what seemed like eternity – but was probably two minutes – pushing hard on a door that clearly said PULL.

Once I was in, a woman showed me to a room and told me to wait. A few minutes later the door opened and in stepped Brian. He was a man whom I had known for years, who had watched me box and even trained with me, so when I saw the horror in his eyes I knew it was born from love.

'Stay here, Ray,' he told me as he swung around and went straight out again. I slumped back and wondered, yet again, how I had ended up here. Was it really because I had smoked a few joints twenty-five years ago?

Brian had clearly been busy because he returned twenty minutes later and informed me that the following morning I would be going to an addiction treatment centre in Luton. A fool could see that it was exactly what I needed – indeed the only thing that could save my life – and yet my first reaction was to think, 'Woah, let's not be too radical here!'

And that is the addict's mind for you. We are a self-pitying bunch when we are suffering, and yet we are often too sick to accept the help that we patently need. 'You want to help take me away from the thing that is killing me? Fuck you!'

This is why many addicts drop out of treatment programmes or fail to turn up for appointments when the threat of serious intervention is levelled. Chronic addicts might make bad decisions but we are not stupid people. In fact, we are master manipulators. We know about the clinical models and how to frustrate well-meaning doctors so much that they end up over-prescribing heroin substitutes such as methadone.

So I considered lying to myself and bullshitting everybody around me yet again ... yet thankfully logic prevailed and I accepted Brian's kind offer. I had run out of road and I knew in my heart that I had nowhere else to go.

Addicts and alcoholics are sentimental creatures who have conveniently selective memories. Before we go into treatment we use one last time, for old times' sake. The drunk sleeping on a park bench, given the option of giving up, will remember the beer garden on a hot summer's day. We love our narcotic comfort blankets.

I was no exception, and I have never been the sort of

addict who lets something as insignificant as having no money get in the way of his using. The night before I began treatment, I managed to manipulate a couple of dealers and get enough of what I needed to keep me from withdrawal until I got to Luton.

The next morning I stuffed a handful of what remained of my possessions into a tatty holdall and readied myself for what lay ahead. I was full of fear as from past experience I knew I was going to go through hell detoxing. But I also knew I had no choice.

A couple of hours later, barely strong enough to carry my own bag, I stepped onto Luton Station. Somebody from the rehab centre was waiting to meet me. I handed him my bag, which pathetically contained a pack of hypodermic syringes. I knew they would be taken from me at the centre, but I just hadn't had the willpower to throw them out myself.

I was in turmoil and terrified. My heart pounded throughout the journey from station to rehab and quickened even further when we arrived and he opened the door to a large concrete building. We ascended a spiral staircase and I heard an unfamiliar noise: laughter.

I sensed that I was in a non-oppressive atmosphere and the people on reception greeted me with warm smiles and congratulated me for having made it there. Next I was taken to an office, but as three women from the counselling team said hello with warm smiles I had an unwelcome moment of clarity.

Surrounded by this wholesomeness and positivity, I realised that I was broken into a million pieces psychologically and my self-esteem was well below basement level. Suddenly I could not bear the world to see me like this and I sat down and crashed my head onto the desk in front of me with a thud.

A woman called Kelly came over to me, stroked my back and assured me I was going to be OK. This human touch caused a strange liquid to well up in my eyes … but not for long. I still had some fight in me to try to scare off the people who were keen to help me.

Another gentle but authoritative female voice addressed me. She introduced herself as Danni Constantinou, and said that she would be my focal counsellor, the one appointed to me. I raised my head from the desk and saw a stunning woman smiling and standing over me.

'Fuck off or I will smash your house up,' I told her. This was the level I had sunk to: I just wanted to reject everybody before they inevitably rejected me. (My chat-up lines clearly also needed a bit of work.)

Why did I say that? I felt so shit about myself right then, and my world was so ugly, that her looks dazzled me like a sun suddenly shining into a cellar. I was the proverbial wounded animal, cornered and prodded with sticks – in this case, the stick of Danni's attractiveness. She was a beauty, and I was certainly the beast.

Humiliated even further after my outburst, I got up from the desk and stormed out of the room like a toddler in the body of a very damaged man. The third counsellor, Candice, followed me out, cooing soothing words of reassurance.

Once again, the kindness in her voice was too much for

me to bear, and alien to a kicked and spurned creature as lost as me. I saw a sofa nearby, staggered over to it and collapsed in an agitated, pitiful heap.

A giant of a man appeared and approached me and without even thinking I clenched my fists, but rather than man-handling me he introduced himself as Terry and tried to calm me down in a language that I could understand. I could tell at once that he came from my world, but all I wanted to do was to escape.

From what?

To what?

Terry was experienced enough to know that I was going into bad withdrawals and he assured me that a doctor was on his way to prescribe a detox. Addicts in need can spot bullshit at fifty paces but I could tell that Terry was telling the truth and, sure enough, a doctor appeared and sorted me out.

Now that I had relief, I settled down and began to interact with my fellow residents. I knew that my journey was about to become very real. Drugs have the effect of dampening negative emotions, but eventually no amount of intoxication can achieve this and our emotional world jumps back and bites us on the arse. Only a real addict will understand this jumping-off point.

No one enters into rehab because they are having a great time. It is the last house on the block for us, and finding yourself there is hard to swallow. It is certainly not a holiday camp.

Having been through treatment before, I had a strong idea of what it was going to be like, but I talked to the other people there and found out from them what to expect. As usual, the treatment model was based around complete abstinence and the twelve-step recovery programme. We would also receive group therapy and individual counselling.

There was also a strong community peer group with other residents in differing stages of recovery. This would prove of paramount importance as peer support is vital. In my experience, a good peer group leads to a much better chance of personal recovery. You see, we are all mad but, thank God, not all at the same time.

The days in the centre were structured in such a way as to encourage us to become disciplined. Patients were only allowed out in groups of three at first, and were expected to attend at least five twelve-step fellowship meetings a week. At nights we stayed in a series of dry houses and were visited by staff and regularly breath- and urine-tested. Far from being oppressive, this was designed to keep us safe.

I was under no illusions and accepted that we needed these boundaries. Addicts in early treatment can be cunning, and the destructive force inside us will push us to the limit given the chance. Having no real knowledge of personal boundaries, we struggle to accept any that are imposed on us.

Yet, untreated, we are so naïve that we don't actually realise we are subconsciously trying to sabotage our own chances of recovery. All too often, addicts in treatment push boundaries so far that they end up being discharged. They rarely stay clean, even when they are so sick that a relapse can lead to their early death.

Very few addicts can accept that by the time they get to rehab they are in the advanced stages of a terminal condition. The forces of denial are strong, and few, if any, of the people who die from overdoses actually believed it would happen to them. I have buried many a good friend to addiction (and my own father, of course).

The clients in the treatment centre were split into two groups named New York and Cleveland. Those two cities were the first ones to see the development of Alcoholics Anonymous.

Cleaveland was run by an excellent counselling psychologist, Candice. I was allocated to New York, run by the beautiful Greek-Cypriot Danni Constantinou, a woman intelligent and shrewd enough to forgive my introductory threat to smash her house up. As my physical state slowly improved, I began to engage well with the group and started to open up with my peers.

Emotionally, I felt raw and afraid as emotions started to flow again and my detox cleared my drug-induced mental fog. I was feeling guilt, remorse, regret, fear, anger, frustration, despair and deep personal loss, although at the time I did not know this.

When Danni first asked me how I was feeling, I said the usual treatment-group mantra: 'I'm feeling fine.' She smiled at me and asked how I really felt.

'I think I feel fine,' I replied. Danni stepped in and pointed out that in those words lies a problem. Non-addicted people will rarely say, 'I think I feel …' They are able simply to feel, and readily identify their emotions. Addicts lack this capacity.

I began by describing to Danni where I was at in life and what being an addict had cost me in terms of consequences. The awful truth was that I had lost everything worthwhile to me, and I could not bear to face up to it. The thought of unlocking the door to my emotions overwhelmed me. I knew that I needed to go to my least favourite place on earth but I was incapable of entering this mental and emotional labyrinth alone.

Danni gently encouraged me to open up the door to my feelings. It proved to be every bit as difficult as I had feared as I struggled to identify what I actually felt. I had built up such impenetrable armour around my emotions that they all appeared as one big ball of hurt.

I simply did not possess the vocabulary to describe what I was feeling at this point. In fact, I don't know even what I felt, only what I thought, and Danni correctly identified this as the crux of my problem.

At this stage, the transition from heart to head was almost instantaneous whenever I had a negative feeling. I would just jump straight back to my twisted thinking, where I felt safer. The trouble was that the addiction lived in my mind and was hugely painful, hence the term – and the desire – to 'get out of my head'. Never once had I said, 'I want to get out of my feelings.'

I agreed with Danni that I wanted to change the way that I felt but the mental process I have just described had always led me back to using and abusing drink or drugs. My mind distorted my ability to reason with my emotions. As an emotional catastrophist – always ready to think the worst – my mind had always amplified any negativity within and led me back into active addiction.

It became obvious now to me that I was struggling to connect emotionally with my thinking. As a result I was acting out impulsively in a variety of destructive manners. My conscious mind had been trying to fix myself in whatever way I could, but subconsciously I had been trying to destroy the part of me that I found the most objectionable. This is the nature of addiction.

What was more, my mind didn't just throw up any sufficient deterrent to stop me from getting another fix. Even if it did, I went through a strange mental process that would always lead me back to the substance of choice or some other form of destructive behaviour.

This had led me in the past genuinely to believe that I could use just once, despite all the evidence to the contrary. These were the complex issues that desperately needed addressing in treatment for me. Denial had defeated me too often in the past, and this time I was finally broken enough to accept the first step of recovery.

I made a clear admission and accepted that I was powerless over my addiction. Now that I had at last reached this point, recovery for me was finally possible.

Obviously, this was not my first time in rehab and I had to ask myself what I was going to do that was so different this time. In the past I had tried on countless occasions to get well, and my greatest hurdle had always been to over-think, psychoanalysing everything to the point of paralysis. I had also listened to many addicts and alcoholics doing the same.

So I recognised that to increase my chances of successful treatment, I needed to lay aside all I thought I knew about recovery and accept help from a power greater than me. This was not going to be an easy task for someone like me.

My personal circumstances had forced me from a very young age to rely on myself to survive. Living by my wits had become a way of coping that I was familiar and safe with. Thank God that this time around my treatments had helped me to concede that I could not think my way out of addiction.

Of course, to get past the denial and defence mechanisms at play within me I had to learn to identify and verbalise my emotions. This took a lot of gentle encouragement from both Danni and Candice. It also took a lot of effort on my part, as it was not easy to risk exposing my vulnerability.

I had come from a criminal world where you trusted only a few people and you certainly did not show any emotion as this was seen as equating to weakness. So for me it was extremely difficult to show people the real Ray Bishop behind the mask.

In any case, I had to find him myself, first.

I was so fortunate to have Danni's support and guidance – she was an excellent therapist. She understood me well and I felt safe in her care. Over the following days and weeks I began to see the futility of many of my twisted beliefs and subsequent behaviours. I began the process of change that, please God, will continue for the rest of my lifetime.

This intervention and treatment took me six months. I had entered that rehab a broken child, and I left there a man with hope in his eyes. I felt my way through the best that I could and I embarked on a lifelong journey of emotional growth.

Today I know that it is OK to feel emotions. I have lost my fear of them. I would go so far as to say I openly embrace them, as I know that they won't kill me. I no longer feel alone as I have a loving fellowship that embraces me, and above all a connection to a God of my own limited understanding.

At last, I have got to where I had needed to be all those years – I have a faith that guides me to do the next right thing, and I follow a programme that demands honesty. It might not sound much, but to me it is the world – and my life.

THE
BEGINNING

I would love to end the story of my life to date by claiming that I am now an accomplished brain surgeon, a beacon of achievement and a role model for people everywhere, but sadly this is not the case.

The real script for my future is as yet unwritten. However, I know that I am venturing into a world more beautiful and rich with possibilities than I could ever have imagined. I finally have something today that no amount of money could ever buy me. I am a free man who believes in himself and I am on the cusp of a sanity I never dreamed possible.

Despite losing the plot so many times over the course of my life, I am lucky that I never totally gave up trying to find a way through and to understand myself. Now I have finally got there, I owe it all to a God of my understanding, the twelve-step programme, and the many people who have helped me along the way.

It has not been all plain sailing since I left treatment two years ago, and I have had to work my way through some lapses and schoolboy errors. I spent a year working again in scaffolding and lost my way for a period. Thankfully I got support and went to a rehab in Coventry for two months to re-evaluate my life.

I was on the same slippery slope as before but came to my senses before the usual thing happened. Once again, I had started to let my recovery slip as I was working seven days a week. My behaviour was becoming addictive once more, but this time I managed to admit it to myself.

It had taken a new form this time. I have always been a real animal lover and I had taken to buying lots of animals. This included a few Shih Tzu dogs and even a collection of horses. People thought I was nuts but I just wanted to care for them.

However, my addictive behaviour and personal insanity had begun to take hold again and I had begun to neglect myself. I was taking too much on and trying to fix myself by creating my own personal farm. Luckily I came to and managed to take a good long look at where I was heading. For the first time, I could see it in crystal clarity.

Taking a deep breath, I found new homes for all of my animals and waved them goodbye. It reduced me to tears as I loved them all so much but I had no choice as I was heading for a fall. Instead, I gave up scaffolding again and went to the rehab in Coventry to spend two months regrouping.

The psychotherapist I worked with, Conner Stagg, helped me to see exactly where I had got it wrong for years. I had never listened to that soft inner resource that was always there. As a result, I got back on track and I am now in a better place than I have ever been mentally and emotionally. Above all I am spiritually alive again and free.

Don't laugh, but I think I am as sane an individual today as you could ever hope to meet. I react normally to situations that used to baffle me. I no longer think criminally and I am certainly not violent in any way. In fact, I have become very soft and gentle and I love helping people.

Today, I spend a lot of my time working with addicts and alcoholics as it reminds me of what I am. I am also repaying in part the many victims I have created in my own addiction throughout the years. My thinking is that if I can help one person to see reason, then my life was not a complete waste of time.

I have been fortunate enough to return to various prisons where I was banged up and give talks on rehabilitation. For me, this is so rewarding. It is a way of carrying hope and also cementing my own commitment towards my recovery.

I have made amends where possible to the people that I have harmed and I continue to do so. I am not perfect by any means, but I am also not the bad person that I once was. The most important change of all is I am no longer as obsessive or angry as I used to be. Today, I really think things through and

I no longer act out impulsively. As long as my connection to a personal higher power is solid on a daily basis, this behaviour has been manageable.

The greatest message that I can carry to anyone is that if I can change then so can you. I have done things that for various reasons I cannot write about in this book. Believe it or not, I have come back from an even darker world than I have described to you.

It has been an extremely long journey for me, with many fuck-ups along the way. Treating me was never going to be easy due to my deep psychopathic tendencies. I could not control the darker side of me, and treatment at times appeared to make me worse.

I know that there is no end to my therapeutic journey or to the spiritual path that I now walk. For me, my only lasting solution has come from finally gaining a higher state of consciousness through engaging totally with the twelve-step programme.

I go to step meetings regularly and I am actively engaged in the fellowship of Narcotics Anonymous. I also attend AA or CA (Cocaine Anonymous) meetings at times. When I am there I am an acquired taste for some, as I speak my mind and do not conform to being brainwashed. Whatever. I have been around long enough to know that healthy recovery is not about becoming a clone who sings someone else's tune.

For me my recovery now is about finding my own identity and accepting those parts of me that in the past were so objectionable. The whole programme is about dependence on a power greater than me. I choose to call that power 'God' but it is my own concept.

Sammy and I split up for a couple of years but I am glad to say we are now back together and better than ever. At the minute I live alone in my own little flat and am comfortable that way, but I see Sam and Poppy a lot. It's like we are in a new relationship, and it's great.

I have even had two boxing matches since I left treatment and I put up a good fight in both. I narrowly lost out on regaining my WCBC British title on a split decision. I lost to the better man on the night but I was still a winner in my eyes. Less than six months before I had been found dead in the road. Win, lose or draw did not really matter – just the fact that I was able to fight again was a victory for me.

I have the respect of my family once again and they are all proud of me. My whole family, my children included, have been amazing in standing behind me in any way they can, and I am pursuing the opportunity to further my psychology studies at university. I hope that through studying further I can one day make a difference to someone's life. Knowledge of my condition has certainly made a difference to mine.

The reality is I do not know where life is going to take me but I pray that it is somewhere positive. All I can do is show up on a daily basis and do the best I can. I have the power of choice today, and I choose wisely.

I am very shrewd in the company I keep and I refuse to let negativity into my life. I avoid loud and abrasive characters and I am blessed with some proper good friends. I have a peace in my heart that is more beautiful than I can describe. I still have my moments, but I am getting better.

To anyone that I ever harmed, I know that a simple sorry will never repair any trauma I caused you. All I can offer you is a prayer for your happiness and wellbeing. I pray that you find every peace and happiness that you would wish for the people you hold closest in your world.

I regret all the pain and chaos I brought to your lives, and if I could change it, I would. I promise you all that I am done with causing suffering and I will now be of service to this world in any way I can.

I still make mistakes – I am only human. I am learning what it means to have relationships today and I do not always get it right. I learn as I go and I do my best to not harm people along the way. I am most certainly no expert in this department and I am yet to meet anyone who is.

Thank you for taking the time to get to know me and I hope that you understand me a bit better now. I most certainly do, and writing this book has undoubtedly been the most rewarding thing I have ever done in my life.

I do not know who you are, but I urge you to face your own personal demons with courage. If you are an addict of my type, get honest and seek help. If you are a criminal as I once was then I urge you to pause and consider your victims. I bid you farewell for now, and thank you for walking with me.

POSTSCRIPT
MY ADDICTION

I believe wholeheartedly that I inherited a genetic pre-disposition for addiction from my father's side of the family. His family was riddled with alcoholism. I was certainly not exposed to it through being nurtured, as he left my life when I was very young. In fact, my mother always warned me of the negative effects of any kind of substance misuse, especially alcohol.

As a result, I was fiercely anti-drinking as a child, but then – like most teenagers – felt compelled to do it anyway. This is why I believe in genetic determinism, as I do not fit most models of straightforward behavioural addiction.

Behaviourism would argue that addiction arises from the repeated pattern of pleasurable experiences until habit occurs. This was certainly not the case for me with many of the substances that I administered to the point of problem use.

I used alcohol at a young age and from the first time did not like it or the way that it affected me. Yet immediately I felt compelled to repeat the behaviour, even though I was not seeking it for its mood-altering quality. Right from the start I knew that I was different for this reason.

I believe my drinking was a form of self-medicating and a type of self-harm. I also know that it was beyond my mental control from the beginning. Whether or not this is down to psychic determinism or not, I am not sure. I do know that I have always been difficult to treat.

I agree that I have had intense psychodynamic conflicts arising from distortions in my psyche. Treating my moral conflicts has proved incredibly difficult owing to the fact that any conflicts were perhaps also influenced by neurological distortions. By this I mean chemical deficiencies in the brain. This factor, along with the environment that I grew up in and was influenced by, could explain why I acted with the behavioural traits of somebody prone to psychotic episodes.

Through self-reflection, I feel I was born with a pathological psychopathy. Drugs tipped the scales for me, as without them psychotic behaviour is not an issue for me. All I can ever hope for is that I continue to manage the symptoms.

For me my drug use was in part a distorted attempt at this. I believe that there are many like me and the warning signs are in part evident in childhood forms of neurosis. I always had deep irrational fears as long as I can remember. I was also incredibly impulsive and obsessive long before I ever took any substances. How much this was down to external forces I do not know. I do know, however, that I can trace them back almost as far as a pre-verbal stage of cognition.

Owing to the psychopathy within me, I often got worse

through different treatments. For example CBT seemed to push me deeper into myself. It was here that I met a new darkness within me and I could not control myself if I felt threatened. I also did not respond well to psychotropic medication as my addictive mind found a way to reason with their effects.

Counselling and other forms of moral intervention helped but I was incapable of putting what I learned into practice. Intense psychotherapy also benefited me as I was able to make strong links within me and bring areas of conflict into my conscious mind. However, the trouble is that is where a large part of the problem lies for me.

I believe that addiction therefore for me is also in some way a spiritual disorder. For a psychotic addict of my description the only real solution is a spiritual approach. This spiritual solution was recognised in the 1930s by Carl Jung. He was one of the first to define alcoholism as a spiritual and psychosomatic disorder. He said that men of my disposition had an insatiable thirst arising from the spirit. Alcoholics Anonymous constructed their twelve-step programme around this theory.

I tend to agree with Jung because I always felt like I had a deep hole in my soul. I believe this arises from the biological aspect of my addiction and that men like me have deficiencies in serotonin levels in the brain. My physiology determined this for me and I tried to fill this hole with drink and drugs for years. It did not work, and I have to come to accept that substance abuse was a symptom of my underlying condition.

By treating my condition through spiritual principles I have been able to achieve and maintain sobriety on a day-to-day basis for quite some time now. Above all I feel whole. The conflict of psychopathy is no longer within me as I have found an inner peace far more powerful than the dark forces that were once beyond my reasoning.

I have conflict resolution in my ego and react in proportion to what life throws at me. I am not foolish enough to believe that I am cured but I do feel that I am finally winning the war. The demon in me has been put to sleep and I have found an effective way to starve him on a daily basis.

Only time will tell if he awakes again but I certainly will continue to do all I can to prevent this. I am no longer fighting myself as I have concluded that it is a fight I can never win. My only choice therefore is to surrender, as it is here that I have finally found peace.

Dr Mich Page
e-mail:

Open Reference for Mr Raymond Bishop

To whom it may concern:
I have been Ray's Open University tutor for the year, 2005, during which time he has been studying a 'Child development' module as part of his Psychology degree programme. Ray is an extremely hard working student, he is intelligent, diligent, punctual and his confidence in his own academic abilities has grown in the time I've known him. His essays and practical work have been of the very highest standards throughout the year, which demonstrates his continued application to his studies as well as his academic abilities.

I have met Ray several times and he is always presentable and seems to get along well with other people. I have always found him cheerful, even when things have been hectic for him or difficult.

I therefore have no hesitation what so ever in recommending him to you, through this open reference, and if I may be of any further assistance, I can be contacted either through the Open University in the South, at Oxford, or via the e-mail address above

Yours sincerely

Dr M G Page

The Hardman Trust
Award Scheme

This is to certify that *a Hardman Trust Award*
has been granted to

Raymond Bishop

In recognition of special commitment to the process of personal rehabilitation

These awards are for men and women serving long sentences in England and Wales
who show a genuine desire to turn their lives around
and work for the good of others and of themselves.

9th June 2006

Lord Woolf
Patron

This award has been made possible through the generosity of the Stone-Mallabar Foundation

ACKNOWLEDGEMENTS

I have so many people to thank who have touched my life in a meaningful way, and I have tried to list them all here. Sincere apologies to anyone who I have inadvertently missed off this list.

Professor David Wilson, Professor L. Cordroy, Dr Mary Bell, Dr J. Mounty, Dr Mitch Page, Dr David Jones, Dr Elizabeth Sullivan, Dr N. Shah, Dr B. Stebbings, Dr J. Marr, Dr A. Smith, Dr P. Bennett, Dr R. Khan.

My Sammy, Danni Constantinou, Noel 'Razor' Smith, Nick and Shaun Kelly, Kath Pike, Paul Johnson, Lorraine Parry, Steve and Carol Spiegel, Jenny Tew, RAPt, Pete McNeaney, Candice Vermooten, Terry Akusu, Kelly Winn, Rosie, Carol and Kim, Conner Stagg, TTP Luton, Providence Project, Quinton House, Henley Court.

Ashley, Leeanne, Anita, Jem Newman and Leigh, Glen Donahue, Chris Cross, Stephen Macdonald, Ray Carrol, Paul Gasgoine, Joe Calzaghe, Steve Holdsworth, Joe Egan, Steve Mitchell, Richard Eve, Peter Gravett, Ricky Abbott, John Arnold, Freddie Lunn, Craig and Lee Finnikin, Tommy Lee,

Paul Fitzgerald, Nick Willis, Jimmy Grant, the Eastwoods, Eddie Smith, Tommy A., Mark D., Kevin B., Danny N., Ian B., Kenny Milne, John Martindale, Darren Hilliard, Big Vic, John James, Eddie, PO Paul Johnson, PO Joe Chapman, Pete Stockwell, Gladeana McMahon, Billy Banks, Nick Hall, K. Withers, Mark Bailey, Neil Price, Sally Barnett, Pat Bryson, Keith and Gary Cable, Toni Smith, Pete Stoten, Roger Dorway, Michael Bourne, Matt and Will, David Fraser, Roger Campbell, Frankie Brooks, Marcel Kelman, Sert, WCBC, Adam, Lloyd Coates, Big Jay, Big Kilps, Stevie E., Oydy Darke, Glen Dale, Max C., Sol, Big Frank, Chris, Colin, Mandy, Caroline, Sinead, Leanne, the McEvoys, Ray B., Kev L., Rookie L., Ray B., Gary S., Martin V., Lennie K., Lenny L., Ollie W., Charlie C., Wilf G., Ray S., Mark S., Lee G., Roderick Reed, Nicky Barton, Terry Morris, Clive Barracks, Bill A., Johnny D., Steve C., Steve R., Lee Murray, Paul Allen, Ben Chalmers, Ben Allen, Brian Massey, Huey Delaney, Jessica Brown, Mark Bailey, Kate O'Conner, Bill Starkey, Phoebe Diane, Stacey Farr and Kelly Farr, Keith and Gary Cable, Danny Nicholson and all those who have touched my life in whatever way. I love and respect you all.

R.I.P.

We will meet again:

Colin Bishop, Arthur Bishop, Betty Bishop, Mazy McEvoy, Patrick McEvoy, Paddy McEvoy, Danny Ware, Jack Shepherd, Big Kev Shepherd, Rob Arnold, Richard Persaud,

ACKNOWLEDGEMENTS

Dean Langford, Ricky Langford, Nicky Gilbert, Terry Carter, John Chamberlain, Dave Chandler, Charlie Smith, Rory Keane, Manchester Ian, Alan Clarke, Mark Strickland, Kevin Logan, Barry Horne, Charlie Kray, Gary Anderson, Michael Rayner, John Williams, Gary Mason, Tony Palmer, Neil H., Dave Jewell, Jamie Beckett, Stevie Goswell, Adam Stevenson, Bobby Honeymoon, Gus, Rico, Nicky, Sharon, Phil, Steve Miller, Micky Skinner, Nicky Payne, Eugine Carter, Roy Shaw, Nicky Stockins, Lenny McClean, Ray Saunders, Dessy Cunningham, Rory Keane, Steve Axam and Biscuit.

May you all sleep well in paradise.

INDEX